A
Countryman's
Year

A Countryman's Year

ALAN C. JENKINS
Illustrated by PETER BARRETT

Webb&Bower

EXETER, ENGLAND

For N.L.W.

Published in Great Britain 1980 by
Webb & Bower (Publishers) Limited,
33 Southernhay East, Exeter, Devon, EX1 1NS

Distributed by WHS Distributors
(a division of W.H. Smith and Son Limited)
St John's House, East Street, Leicester, LE1 6NE

Designed by Peter Wrigley

Copyright © Text: Alan C. Jenkins 1980
Illustrations: Peter Barrett

British Library Cataloguing in Publication Data

Jenkins, Alan Charles
    A countryman's year.
    1. Country life – Great Britain
    2. Natural history – Great Britain
    I. Title
    941'.00973'4   DA667

    ISBN 0–906671–17–5

Phototypeset in Great Britain by
Filmtype Services Limited, Scarborough, Yorkshire

Printed and bound in
Hong Kong by Mandarin Publishers Limited

By the same author:

White Horses and Black Bulls
Between the Two Twilights
Dear Olga
Kingdom of the Elephants
Wild Swans at Suvanto
Storm over the Blue Hills
The Golden Band
A Wealth of Trees
Shadow of the Deer
Wildlife in Danger
The Naturalists

HALF-TITLE PAGE: A curlew on its
nest. One egg has already hatched.

TITLE PAGE: Combine harvesters at
work near Streatley Warren.

Contents

May

June

July

August

September

October

November

Introduction

A Countryman's Year is neither a diary nor a chronicle of the twelve months. To record everything encountered or seen or heard in the countryside throughout the year would be impossible – every time you set foot outside something presents itself that is worthy of notice – the wheeling of the stars, the weather portents in the sky, the first aconite, the first bean shoots poking up in the garden, a sparrowhawk beating the lanes, the hatching of a brood of chicks, the seasonal work of farming neighbours, bird-table antics, a river in spate – with every new day there is something to record.

But to attempt to put it all down in a book such as this, even if it were possible, would make for a sedulous and unwieldy catalogue of monotonous character. So I have simply presented some of the happenings, things, phenomena, activities, that have struck me, pleased me, amused me: maybe it could be called a personal pastiche. Most of the pieces are expanded versions of the notes I keep – the telegraphese notes themselves would have been too brief here.

And, incidentally, note-taking is one of the pleasantest activities for a naturalist or country-dweller (and for that matter for the townsman in a different sphere – Pepys became immortal through keeping a diary!), while it is an absolute essential for anyone professing an interest in nature. Like the colours of a hooked fish, the human memory fades with terrible swiftness – not only fades, but becomes distorted.

I live on Dartmoor, but this book is not about that region, nor does it portray any particular region: the scenes and incidents are from near and far, mainly round about my own home, but also from other parts of the country which I happened to visit. Most of the natural history in it could have occurred almost anywhere.

A little of the material in the book originally featured in *The Times*, *The Birmingham Post*, *Blackwood's Magazine*, *The Month*, *Wildlife* and the BBC European Service, and I take this opportunity of making the usual acknowledgements.

It is a great pleasure and privilege to have Peter Barrett's evocative paintings as illustrations for this book.

January

The Saxons are said to have called January 'Wolf-month' because wolves devoured most of their human victims then. There were certainly many wolves in England at that time, for much of the country was still covered in forest, giving them ample protection. The *Brut y Tywysogion* records that the tenth-century King Edgar, first king of All-England, exacted from one of his vassal princes a yearly tribute of three hundred wolfskins. This tribute was reportedly paid for half a century, which would have entailed the slaughter of some fifteen thousand wolves.

January can indeed be a hungry month, and at times during harsh weather, with the fields burnt by the frost, the woods sullen and lifeless, the streams curling and twisting as if in agony beneath sheaths of ice, the spirit of the wolf seems to lurk everywhere, so that at twilight especially one's homeward pace quickens imperceptibly through deep-banked, tree-gloomy lanes. It is good to climb on to higher, franker ground where a purple light still tinges the smattering of snow. One no longer quite feels, in George Meredith's words, that

> *Thousand eyeballs under hoods*
> *Have you by the hair.*

Redolent of all this is the sonorous lowing of hungry cattle, a menacing and disturbing sound full of strange undertones expressive of Man's age-long struggle for food. It is as if this throaty 'murgling' is to remind us not only of the cattle's own hunger, but of how tenuous is our hold on the few inches of soil that provide us with our food. In spite of modern butter mountains and beef mountains we have never from one generation to another been able to take our resources for granted.

Because he had to fetch the vet to his ailing pony, my neighbour Mr Maddowcroft was late feeding his cattle, bullocks and dry cows, and I gave him a hand humping bales of hay, seventy pounds apiece, the binder twine cutting into the hands, the knees awkwardly levering the great oblong bundles. I remembered the huge, cumbersome hay-knife we used in the days before baling took over. You climbed on a ladder into the heart of the rick and thrust the knife in with a satisfying crunching and cut out wadges of rich, closely packed hay the colour of tobacco and as rich in scent.

As soon as we drove down over the crest of the sloping lane, with the pattern of the tyres rolling out on the thin snow as if from a printing machine, we could see the cattle in the distance tallucking excitedly towards the field gate. They would scarcely let us through and pranced and cavorted alongside the trailer as we threw off the bales, whose fragrance brought memories of summer to the January evening when the cold was already making the nostrils tingle, and dragonlike clouds of vapour poured from the muzzles of the animals and the coverlet of snow crackled lightly under the wheels of the puttering tractor. In spite of the diesel fumes John Clare's vivid lines came to mind:

> *The foddering boy along the crumping snows*
> *With straw-band-belted legs and folded arm*
> *Hastens, and on the blast that keenly blows*
> *Oft turns for breath, and beats his fingers warm,*
> *And shakes the lodging snows from off his clothes,*
> *Buttoning his doublet closer from the storm*
> *And slouching his brown beaver o'er his nose –*
> *Then faces it agen, and seeks the stack*
> *Within its circling fence where hungry lows*
> *Expecting cattle, making many a track*
> *About the snow, impatient for the sound*
> *When in huge forkfuls trailing at his back*
> *He litters the sweet hay about the ground*
> *And brawls to call the staring cattle round.*

We didn't have to call the cattle. They trampled half the hay in their excitement before seizing it in eager mouthfuls and throwing it about to separate it out, while one old black matron continued to low hoarsely as if emphasizing to the others that it was her efforts which had summoned up the farmer.

But the work wasn't finished yet. The sheep had to be fed, too, so we went and opened up a root-clamp skilfully thatched with straw and covered with soil. The fat, opulent-looking, golden-orange swedes lay in it like treasure in some ancient tomb so that it seemed almost wrong to loot them.

'Better nor turmuts,' declared Mr Maddowcroft. 'Swedes has less water in 'em. Turmuts spoil too easy in the frost. Won't keep.'

He gave me a couple of swedes to take home. They are delicious, diced and steamed, and will last us a week or two.

*

As well as its wolfish character, there is an austere beauty about January, ironically rendered more impressive the worse the weather happens to be. And the tree is one of its most impressive features: the tree, the deciduous tree, in full leaf is lovely enough, sighing, it sometimes seems, under that burden of rippling green

in which all manner of life goes on, from the turtle-dove uttering its endless, soothing, purring praise of summer, to the myriad otherworld of insects seething in the bark.

But in midwinter the intricate, awe-inspiring architecture of the branches is revealed in all its soaring grandeur and must surely have been an inspiration to the ancient masons when they built the cathedrals. The fan-vaulting of an Exeter is like some eternal tree climbing skyward; the massy columns of a Durham are like the sturdy boles of oak or beech. Nor is this especially fanciful; after all, the first temples were the groves of hilltop trees and the Druids worshipped the oak; indeed, their name is said to mean simply 'oak-men'.

Most thrilling of all is the sight of some great tree limned against the night sky, with stars netted in that stupendous filigree of twigs and branches. At the same time one marvels at the thought of the life-giving sap drawn from the all-nourishing earth and rising to the utmost tip of the highest twig.

It is often imagined that sap rises and falls according to the seasons. But there is always sap in the tree; otherwise the tree would die. It is true, however, that in spring the sap does flow more strongly; it is also true that the only living parts of the tree consist of the ends of the roots, the leaves and the buds, and, further in from the outer bark, the sapwood and phloem. The sapwood and phloem perform the continuing function of carrying the life-giving sap, the chemicals and minerals, to create the new sapwood the tree is pushing out all round its girth every year. As the tree grows, the original sapwood dries out and

Bertrand Russell once said that mathematics possessed a beauty cold and austere. So too does winter.

hardens, largely through the influence of tannin, a vegetable substance contained in the tree which has very astringent qualities. And this becomes true wood or xylem, the heartwood which is the real timber but which is in effect now dead.

Mute Swans, tufted duck and mallard resigned to the bitter immobility of winter.

*

At the foot of the trees and in contrast with their majesty is the snowdrop, flower of the month if ever there was one. It is a gentle miracle of the winter, nodding delicately, wonderfully unscathed by the most wolfish of weather. Frail-looking, faintly green-flecked, it seems almost dreamily unreal as it huddles under bleak hedgerows. Its clusters are tiny beacons of hope, for you must be pretty hard-boiled not to be gladdened by seeing them.

Yet this flower, so redolent of the English winter, is not a native of England. The earliest reference to it in the *Oxford English Dictionary* is dated 1664: 'Those purely white flowers that appear about the end of winter, and are commonly call'd a Snow Drop.' Shakespeare didn't know the snowdrop – at least, he never mentions it, which surely he would have done otherwise. (But neither, for that matter, does he mention that other marvellous English flower, the foxglove.)

The wild snowdrop is supposed to have escaped from monastery gardens and certainly it spreads easily enough. Its little brown bulbs are often scattered by blackbirds foraging desperately among the dead leaves and the moss. The blackbirds do not scratch, they do not know how to, any more than wild birds in general except for the jungle fowl, ancestor of barnyard poultry. But they scuff with their beaks and displace a surprising amount of material in so doing. So perhaps as well as for his mellow, leisured song, we are indebted to the blackbird for helping to spread this charming flower whose colour admirably sets off his own as he flips aside the debris of the banks and hedges.

*

Perhaps because later in the year there is far more natural activity about the countryside, the sounds of January are often more noticeable individually and in some cases more dramatic. The robin utters his friendly, wistful thread of song, often prompted by the arrival of a human being. Or wistful-*sounding* one perhaps ought to say, not wishing to be accused of anthropomorphism. The missel-thrush pours forth his wild, spasmodic, ringing defiance from a topmost branch – Meredith's stormcock.

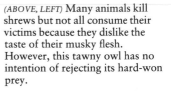

...who sings me, out of winter's throat
The young time with the life ahead.

The estuaries echo with the liquid, silver chorus of teeming waders, the lovely *too-luie* of grey plover, the lament of redshank, bark of godwit, grunting undertone of knot, ringing cries of oyster-catchers, incomparable nostalgic querying note of curlew.

Among the most evocative sounds to be heard in January are the night-time cries of foxes. For they are supremely active in midwinter, not merely because of hunger but because this is their mating-season. Their eerie calls, especially the gasping scream of the vixen, induce an atavistic shiver and one is suddenly transported back through thousands of years to the days when our distant ancestors huddled round a fire and harkened with dread to the voices of the wild.

But for me, one of the most 'atmospheric' sounds of the January night is the hooting of tawny owls. Sometimes I have seen one of our local owls sitting on a branch of the neighbouring beech-trees, silhouetted dimly, while in the distance a quavering, almost bubbling hoot can be heard; the owl in the tree responds and a duet follows, owl answering owl until presently the owl in the tree glides out into the night, dreamlike in its silence, and the hooting changes to the sharper flight-call of *kiwak kiwak*.

To Man, lost in the night, and still basically afraid of the dark, owls have always been objects of superstitious beliefs, because of their nocturnal habits, their sepulchral cries, and their liking for ancient towers as Macbeth knew. 'It was the owl that shrieked, the fatal bellman which gives the stern'st good-night.' It

(ABOVE)
Is this the wilderness that Cowper
longed for

*Where rumour of oppression and
 deceit,
Of unsuccessful or successful war,
Might never reach me more?*

used to be thought that the screech of the barn owl, for example, was part of its hunting technique, causing its prey to reveal itself. But in fact the small animals in question, 'the wee, sleekit, cow'rin, tim'rous beasties', are more likely to freeze than obligingly reveal themselves.

Certainly the owl's eyes are far better adapted for night-vision than are ours. (Tribes in Northern India used to eat the eyeballs of owls in the hope of acquiring similar powers.) The sensitivity of their retina is a hundred times greater than that of human eyes, but set against this is the fact that the owl's eyes cannot move in their sockets; the bird is obliged to turn its head to see anything out of the direct line of vision. To make up for this it can turn its head through more than 180 degrees.

On a bright moonlight night an owl will hunt by sight, but it is simply not possible for it to see in complete darkness. The owl relies far more on its power of hearing, which is exceptionally acute. This is supplemented by its very thick soft plumage which makes possible its unique silent, ghostly flight.

Now the tawny owls are hunting far away across the frost-rimed meadows and their questioning ululation grows faint as a memory. Some would say that by their persistent hooting (what an ungracious word for such a lovely sound) they are asserting their hunting territory; it always seems to me more likely that they are calling to reassure each other of their continued company.

*Sweet Suffolk owl, so trimly dight
With feathers, like a lady bright,
Thou sing'st alone, sitting by night,
Te whit! Te whoo! Te whit! To whit!
Thy note that forth so freely rolls
With shrill command the mouse controls;
And sings a dirge for dying souls
Te whit! Te whoo! Te whit! To whit!*

Thus Thomas Vauton wrote in the early seventeenth century. In *Birds and Man* W. H. Hudson put it like this:

*A single, long, uninflected note and after it a silent
interval of eight or ten seconds; then the succeeding
longer, much more beautiful note, quavering at first, but
growing steady and clear, with some slight modulations
in it. The symbols* hoo-hoo *and* to-wit to-who, *as
Shakespeare wrote it, stand for the wood (tawny) owl's
note in books; but you cannot spell the sound of an oaten
straw, nor of the owl's pipe. There is no* w *in it, and no* h
and no t *. It suggests some wind instrument that
resembles the human voice, but a very un-English one —
perhaps the high-pitched somewhat nasal voice of an
Arab intoning a prayer to Allah. One cannot hit on the*

precise instrument, there are so many; perhaps it is
obsolete, and the owl was taught his song by lovers in the
long ago, who wooed at twilight in a forgotten tongue,

And gave the soft winds a voice,
With instruments of unremembered forms.

But January is a hard time for owls. Their chief prey, rats, bank-voles and field-voles, lie close as can be in the burning cold, and the woodmice creep into the houses, preferably some cosy apple-loft with all the comforts any mouse could desire. However, notwithstanding the short commons they endure in midwinter owls are the most valuable of birds to the farmer, and provide constant evidence of their useful work. For unlike other predatory birds such as the hawks, they do not skin or tear their prey. They swallow it whole, subsequently disgorging the indigestible parts in so-called pellets, neat little packages the size of a walnut. In one piece of investigation 700 owl pellets were examined and found to contain the remains of 2,513 mice. Another expert survey calculated that five pairs of barn owls in a square mile area were eating close on 24,000 rats, mice and other rodents a year.

No wonder Charles Waterton threatened to strangle his gamekeeper if he molested the resident tawny owls!

*

But it is not only the owls that are discountenanced by a hard winter. Nature in general is sometimes put out of joint, as in a memorable year such as 1963, which was worse than that of 1979 though memories of the latter, being closer in time, remain more vivid. In Scotland, red deer by the thousand flocked down from the hillside in search of food, and poachers made the most of the opportunity, preferably dazzling the animals by the light of car headlamps and shooting them down.

Cold cold!
Cold tonight is broad Moylurg,
Higher the snow than the mountain range,
The deer cannot get at their food.

It was a bleak time for all wild creatures and fatal to many. It was the coldest winter recorded in central and southern England for more than two hundred years. Freezing fog covered the trees with thick bracelets and sheaths of ice. Many beaches froze up entirely, often to as much as four hundred yards below high-tide mark, and some sheltered bays were frozen solid. It seemed as if a new ice age was coming.

Worst off were the birds. Those which could, fled before it. Huge flocks went flying past, big enough to show up on radar

A dormouse feeding on hawthorn berries. In January it will be soundly asleep having stored enough fat in its body to carry it through to spring.

screens and be filmed. Lapwings and skylarks, blackbirds and linnets, corn buntings and greenfinches, the panic-wings rushed by. Even birds that come to Britain every winter from Scandinavia, such as fieldfares, redwings, bramblings, were forced to fly farther south; even birds that do not usually migrate, such as herons, had to move on or face death by starvation and numbing frost. But here was an irony – Northern Europe suffered from the same bitter winter, so that while birds were fleeing from Britain, others were fleeing north across the Channel to our shores, bewildered by the iron-hard weather.

It was then that the humble bird-table proved its worth. It became more than just a stage for the blue tits and great tits to perform their acrobatics on the bag of nuts or chaffinches and nuthatches to glare at each other. As that fearful winter developed, many strange guests, which in normal times would not come anywhere near a house, were glad to accept the bounty provided. In one place even partridges were observed feeding underneath a bird-table on food scattered by other visitors. Tree-creepers, snipe, jays, woodpeckers, skylarks, sea-gulls – these were only a few of the unusual supplicants seen by kitchen-window observers. A fieldfare was seen pecking at an

'The sedge has withered from the lake, And no birds sing . . .' The kingfisher contemplates the winter pond. If it freezes over he will find it very difficult to survive.

orange while somewhere else a moorhen developed a taste for cat food.

Other visitors took advantage of all this, to prey on the birds feeding at the bird-tables. There were several instances of little owls and kestrels swooping down and seizing members of the bread-line. Nevertheless, those homely bird-tables saved hundreds of avian lives.

Of all the birds perhaps the worst off in a hard winter is the kingfisher, the most beautiful English bird, a gaudy cobalt and emerald and bright chestnut jewel of a creature which plunges into the water after tiny fish, flips them in the air and swallows them head first. When the rivers freeze over, the kingfisher is cut off from its food supply, so it flies long distances down to the sea-shore to try its luck. But that is fruitless if the shore-line freezes too far out for the kingfisher to pounce on its prey. In 1963 the species suffered considerably and was wiped out in parts of the country.

✻

These cattle in Northamptonshire are being fed on turnips and other root crops to supplement the grass which at this time of the year is both scarce and less nutritious.

Not all Nature is caught out by the cold. Many creatures, butterflies, bees, lizards, snakes, frogs, avoid the rigours of winter simply by opting out and going to sleep. Some of the mammals, too: bats hang in clusters in church-tower, cave or barn, the dormouse rolls itself into a ball with its thickly-furred, long tail wrapped right round its body and over its head and falls into a profound slumber. A hard winter suits the dormouse best, for if the season is too mild it wakes up when food is still scarce. The hedgehog, fat like the dormouse from good autumn feeding, makes a bed of leaves and moss in some cosy hedgeside nook and snores contentedly during the worst of the cold.

'Hibernation' simply derives from the Latin for winter. It is a natural process that enables certain animals to pass an otherwise difficult period without the effort of seeking food. The action of the animal's heart diminishes considerably; breathing is minimal. A hibernating animal appears dead; indeed, it is very near death. It exists on the fat tissue stored up in its body and on waking again at the end of the winter is much thinner and lighter in weight. Arthur Thompson recorded a female dormouse which weighed 510 grains in September, while on the 10 March following her weight was exactly 300 grains.

Contrary to popular belief the squirrel, red or grey, does not hibernate. Like the bank-vole and other rodents, it will bury food, such as hazel-nuts, though whether it ever retrieves these is open to doubt, as you can frequently discover little caches here and there. Nor does the badger hibernate. Like all animals it dislikes dirty weather and will if necessary miss out a night or two's hunting, even in a wet spell, let alone snow. Although it does not hibernate, it can go for long periods without food and a remarkable instance of this was recorded sixty years ago, by Fairfax-Blakeborough in *Life and Habits of the Badger*.

When the late Tom Green had a string of horses in training at Hambleton, he and his hind [bailiff] one day saw the track of

(ABOVE, LEFT) The grey squirrel does not hibernate, but it stokes up for winter by increasing its food intake in the autumn. Many of the hazel-nuts it buries in mossy crevices lie forgotten and the springtime warmth causes them to germinate.

a badger in the snow. This was about Christmas Day, and on following the badger to his home among the rocks they set a trap and walled it in very tight so that Brock had to come out into the trap or, as the only alternative, starve to death inside. For no less a period than fourteen weeks the badger refused to take the trap, but then he abdicated and was taken alive. He was found to be very thin, at which one cannot wonder.

Indeed, no!

❋

The snow is the census sheet of the wild. The birds are always prompt in filling it in and you can soon see the delicate tracery of their claws as they forage here and there in evident bewilderment. Sometimes there is the sweeping pattern of wing-tips as a larger

(ABOVE) Fox on ice. It is not easy to distinguish between dog-fox and vixen. In general the dog-fox is bigger, reaching a weight of fifteen pounds, the vixen is a few pounds lighter and sometimes has a narrower face.

bird, crow or buzzard, has stooped down at the surface. Underneath the bird-table is a maze of tracks where robin, dunnock and chaffinch have searched for yesterday's crumbs.

But the mammals are much tardier in making their mark. As far as they are concerned, for the first day, even two days, the snow lies unsullied and silent, an immaculate shroud covering an apparently dead world. However, the animals are there all right; they just abominate bad weather. The badger lies curled up in its sett; the rabbit huddles in its burrow; the fox wraps its brush more tightly over its muzzle, though the cry of the vixen will set it twitching. Presently, though, hunger begins to prick more than the cold does. Suddenly there is a tangle of tracks where previously you had thought nothing stirred.

It is a dramatic revelation that makes you realize how much must go on without your being aware of it. Night after night the wild animals go about their lawful occasions, but grass and heather do not betray them as the snow does – though here and there, perhaps by a river's edge, mud or sand do. The smaller the mammal, the less evident its tracks, and in any case all who can have harboured up snugly with food-caches near by. If woodmice are abroad in the snow, their tail marks show, whereas rat and house mouse seem to keep their tails lifted slightly. Weasels, weighing maybe one hundred grammes, leave barely discernible traces, appropriate to their mincing, delicate action. Squirrels – you can track them in park or garden – often leave all four pad-marks together, the hind ones larger and emphatically splayed out.

The most easily recognizable tracks are those of rabbits, the familiar two big, two small, as they lollop along. For as it runs, the rabbit drops its forepaws first then makes a leap-frogging action over their marks, as does the hare, though needless to say the hare's tracks are bigger and more widely spaced. Moreover, the hare often takes enormous leaps, twelve feet or more, to break its trail.

The longer the snow lasts, the more criss-crossed the rabbit spoor becomes, sometimes giving the impression that there are far more rabbits than is the case. Drama is implicit when I come across the unmistakable tracks of a fox and suddenly the deeper, scuffed tracks as the chase began. The trail leads over a bank; just beyond it the snow is sullied and churned, with a significant patch of pink blood, traces of fur, and the dirt of death.

A fox's tracks are not always easy to distinguish from those of a dog. It is usually a matter of size – most dogs are clumsier, heavier than the fox. But both animals show two claw-marks at the top of the print, with the others at the sides of the pads. However, there is one big difference – the fox's track shows up as a straight line of single footprints; he has the knack of placing his hind-paws exactly in the tracks of his forefeet. A badger's claws are much more grouped together at the top of the pad, while the tracks of a cat are unmistakable, for they do not show any claw-marks.

Many years ago I used to keep, or try to keep, a record of animal tracks, at first by making rough drawings of them on the spot. Then I graduated to taking plaster casts of them, needless to say not in the snow but in soft earth or mud. There is considerable skill in this which I never seemed to acquire and my efforts looked more like the tracks of a crippled were-wolf than those of any living creature.

The expert tracker can read the prints of animals as fluently as the ordinary person can read a book. I used to know an old 'harbourer' in the New Forest (his job was to indicate to the hunt where a suitable stag or buck was harbouring) who could tell the size, age, sex and speed of a deer from its spoor. But even the tracks of sheep or cattle evoke a response in one's make-up. Perhaps the age-old, shadowy hunter that still exists within us stirs at the sight.

February

Down in the chalk valleys the lights are disappearing. The villages are sleeping. Up on the hillside the shepherd's work is beginning. For weeks the old man will be isolated during the lambing of the flock, his only company the unquiet ewes, his Welsh sheepdog, the hare, and the prowling fox. Now and then he will be able to walk down to his cottage in the hollow for a while, but February will long have turned before he sleeps in it again. During these long, often bitter nights his home is a corrugated-iron wheeled hut, his bed a few sacks of meal.

The material reward for this labour and discomfort is not much; but pride in his work, love for his charges, are no small part of his recompense. If ever a man was proud of his work and contented in it, the shepherd is. He is a craftsman, his work is his life. It doesn't concern him one whit that he owns not a single ewe among the hundreds he tends. What makes him different from other workers? Is it the romantic aura with which we envelop him? Or is it perhaps that the job has a mellowing influence on men who follow it? Long hours of solitude on the placid downs or hills have a tranquillizing effect; either a man can't stand the life or it makes him meditative, and constant association with the sheep who depend on him makes him efficiently calm and unhurried.

Something had disturbed the ewes when I walked up the deep-gouged beech-track to join the shepherd under the starlight; they answered each other's tremulous bleatings, primordial fear aroused by the coming of night, so that the dog shivering outside the pens became a wolf again. Within the sack-and-straw padded hurdles the shepherd made his rounds, his lantern bobbing here and there, a glow-worm in the hedgerow of night, his grotesque shadow stalking him but never catching up. It was not merely imagination that made the ewes seem to grow calmer as he spoke to them. Their eyes turned to brief diamonds in the light.

The old man plodded across the straw-strewn enclosure. For the time being all was well. He could snatch an hour or two's rest before the first-born of the flock arrived. He clambered into the hut – cluttered with sacks and paint-pots, a small medicine chest, crook and bottles – and cut bread and cheese and took a golden onion from a string. With his Wessex drawl, which sometimes rose comically in a querulous note as he laboured a point, his watchful eyes, his theatrical Newgate fringe, his powerful nose,

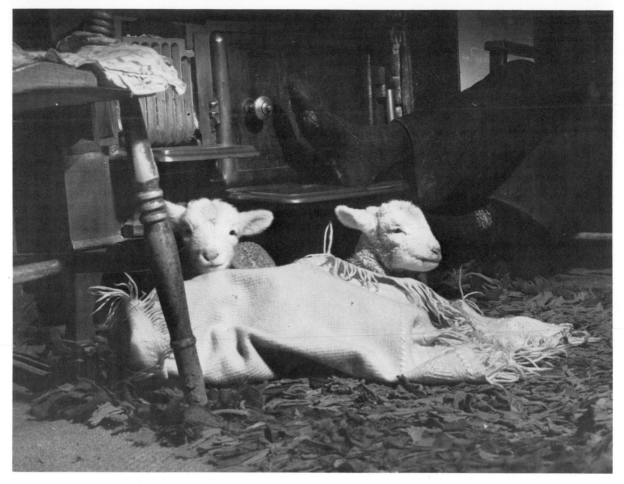

Every year many lambs have to be brought in to the warmth of the farmer's kitchen where they are reared on the bottle. No doubt the farmer's wife hopes that they'll soon be strong enough to go out into the fields, for feeding them is a demanding job.

his smooth cheeks tanned – polished almost – a light mahogany by sun and wind and rain, he was such a man as Hardy might have taken as a model. Presently, when he stoked the little stove and the atmosphere became increasingly throat-catching, I thought of Gabriel Oak in *Far from the Madding Crowd,* and how he was nearly suffocated one lambing night. Here was another Oak, grown into vigorous and proud old age. But his Bathsheba was a much less flighty character – and she made the most marvellous bramble-pies I have ever tasted, the pastry always handsomely glazed.

The stars had not moved very far when the shepherd rose from his couch of sacks, donned his cape and apron of hessian, and went out into the glassy wind. Here and there a low, protesting bleat and the stir of an uneasy body in the straw emphasized the silence of the downs, a silence so profound that it could be felt, heard. The mind had difficulty in believing such a silence, and one listened for something beneath its surface. The looming ridge of downland was like a great dream-ship ploughing on into a calm sea and the stars were the riding lights of who knows what celestial craft.

Out of the darkness came the old man's voice, soothing, enquiring. The bobbing lantern halted and was lowered. Presently it rose again, and the shepherd approached, in his arm a dim, two-headed bundle, all legs which in a day or two would be kicking and running races in the winter grass: the first-born of the flock, the twins, or doubles as he called them.

'Look yur,' he announced triumphantly, 'thur's a good sign. The first-born is doubles. Idden that propshus, now? But they bin born nigh on an hour, and that's bad shepherden: sleepen while my ship's a-labouren. Zno what the Book says about such goings-on? It says: "Woe to the idle shepherd that leaveth his flock. His arm shall be clean dried up and his right eye shall be utterly darkened!" I read that out in church back along from the lectern, and parson told me I'd got a good strong delivery. Tarrible hard words, but just. Howbe,' he went on, straightening up from settling the new family in a hurdle-coop, 'I don't feel no dryen up in my right arm nor yet my left – though the dratted mugwort'll get me in summer agen and make I swell up.'

He went back across the pen, pleased at the 'propshus' sign. When he returned he had another 'sign' – a jet-black lamb. This time no ewe followed trustingly at heel; the mother was dead. He took the newborn lamb into the hut and rubbed it down with a wisp of hay, then prepared the bottle with which the orphan would have to be content until a foster-mother was found. And persuaded, for it takes guile to get a ewe to accept a strange lamb.

'A blessen that black veller didden come first, zno?' the shepherd confided, as he coaxed the lamb. 'I don't vancy unwolesome signs. If you start well you end well, and they doubles was a good start for the flock. When we yawled up thiccy hut over the chalk, I heard whisht-hounds crossing the sky, yelling like a pack of hound-whelps down in the kennels, and one of 'em loitered, for I heard the crack of a whip, and I didden like that. But as 'tis they've done no hurt.'

'Wild geese,' I suggested.

He bedded the lamb down in a nest of straw and stood up.

'Ah, that's what you all say, master likewise. An old man's vancies. But there's more to it than that. We all likes to be comforted, we're that faint-hearted, and there's more folk about believe in signs than 'ood care to admit!'

The pattern of crow's feet round his eyes expanded into a complicated network as he took up the lantern. He liked to indulge in his signs and portents and half the fun was in making other people believe he meant it all.

He stood under the starlight among his ewes, watching the sky and sniffing the wind that came bluffing over the wiry turf of the downs. Before dawn it would drop and there would be a touch of frost; but that was better than rain any day. He went stooping off on his rounds of midwifery.

Now, all that took place before the last war when as a youth I used to stay on a Wiltshire farm. I went there again recently. That

Hudson's description of Shepherd Bawcombe is as apt today as when it was first written: 'There's as much individual difference among dogs as there is in men; but if the breed is right, and you go about it the right way, you can hardly fail to get a good servant.'

(LEFT)
Let us walk in the white snow
  In a soundless space;
With footsteps quiet and slow,
  At a tranquil pace,
    Under veils of white lace.

(ABOVE) An isolated shepherd's cottage on Ickornshaw Moor, Yorkshire. The shepherd needs to be independent in character for, by the nature of his calling, he is often cut off from other men.

(ABOVE RIGHT) Where there's muck, there's money, it's said. Certainly there is nothing like it for the land. Here it is being spread on a field of stubble.

old shepherd's grandson is now in charge, himself a man of middle years. At lambing-time he lives in a motor-caravan instead of a hut. Proprietary medicines line the shelves instead of time-worn remedies. In slack times the shepherd consoles himself with a transistor and has a liking for *'Any Questions?'* Otherwise nothing is changed and there is the same pervasive atmosphere of calm and control, an almost mystical tranquillity and confidence.

The shepherd has always been the most romantic character in farming. Biblical associations are of course partly responsible – shepherds watching their flocks by night, the image of Christ as shepherd, the shepherd himself representing wisdom and loving care, with the lamb as the symbol of innocent new life. But there is something atavistic – albeit unconsciously – about our attitude, too. For the shepherd is by far the oldest figure in agriculture: he represents man's first advance from being purely a hunter. The sheep was domesticated much earlier than cattle or pig and far earlier than the horse. Only the devilish goat among the farm animals can claim as ancient a link with Man.

✳

Cabbage-month seems a churlish nickname for February, but that, according to Verstegan, the seventeenth-century author of *'Restitution of Decayed Intelligence'* (to give his book its quaint title) is what the Saxons called it. 'They named February *Sprout-kele* [alias Colewort], because this was the first vegetable which in that month began to yield out wholesome young sprouts.'

Other authorities scoffed at such an interpretation, claiming that February was called *Sol-monath,* not because the suffix had anything to do with the sun, but because Sol meant mire or mud, and is the origin of the word sully. But Mire-month is not

(RIGHT) Headley Heath, Surrey: frost, fog and snow combine to produce a magical landscape.

(RIGHT) Headley Heath, Surrey: frost, fog and snow combine to produce a magical landscape.

(LEFT) A common winter sight: the deeply rutted mud track to a farm.

necessarily an accurate nickname for February, any more than is February Fill-dyke, for twice as much rain falls in January or August. That Elizabethan chronicler of farm life and methods, Thomas Tusser, qualified it when he said

February, fill the dyke,
With what thou dost like.

With what thou dost like – therein lies the difference. Depending on the weather, the dykes or ditches in February can be equally stuffed with snow or full of melt-water from it or sealed with ice or gurgling with rain-water, to the discomfort of any hedgehog harbouring in the leaf-mouldy bottom. The month can be either the prolongation of winter, to which January opened the door, or it can provide the first fitful chink of spring, presaged by hazel catkins or the green spikes of cuckoo-pint – which look appropriately like tightly-furled umbrellas.

That same Verstegan catalogued all the names he claimed the Saxons had given to the months. As we have seen, one of the most evocative names was Wolf-month for January – though there has never been a fully authenticated case of wolves

The music of the winter estuaries is among the loveliest sounds in nature. When the tide goes out the table is spread once more.

attacking human beings in normal circumstances. But of course it is much more dramatic to think of their doing so, as in the story of the last wolf to be killed in Britain.

In 1743 a wolf was reported in the north-east Highlands, and when it killed two children the Laird of MacIntosh ordered a *tainchel* or drive to which was summoned a renowned hunter, MacQueen of Pall'-a'-chrochain, a giant of a man 6 feet 7 inches tall. Next day, however, when the tainchel met, MacQueen failed to appear and precious time was lost. When eventually he turned up, flanked by his hunting-dogs, the laird reproached him angrily. *'Ciod e a' chabhag?'* ('What was the hurry?') MacQueen responded insolently. MacIntosh and his men reacted fiercely to such an attitude, whereupon MacQueen drew back his plaid and revealed the bloody head of the wolf. *'Sin e dhuibh!'* ('There it is for you!'), he said, flinging it down at their feet.

March was named dramatically, too, according to other authorities, being known as Fierce-month, because of the winds that often herald its entry like the proverbial lion. May, more romantically, was *Thri-mylce* or *Tri-milki,* in other words the month during which, because of the lush pasture and the long hours of sunlight, the cows could be milked three times a day, a practice which continued into modern times in renowned dairy regions such as Cheshire. Surprisingly perhaps, *'tri-milki'* is the only farming allusion in that ancient inventory.

June and July were both named *Litha,* the warm months. July was long ago one of the prettiest names of the months, for it used to be accented Júly, instead of Julý as now. August was *Weōd-monath,* which will be appreciated by gardeners, for it meant 'Weed-month'. September was *Halig-monath,* Holy month, an important time for sacrifice to gods and idols, sublimated nowadays in our Harvest Home thanksgivings. But the ancients made doubly sure, November also being a month of sacrifice, *Blōt-monath.*

Before that in October rough weather had laid low many of the forest trees, so it was known as *Winter-fylleth* or Storm-felling month. As for December, it was of course Yule, but *Se aeria Geola,* the 'former' Yule to distinguish it from January which was *Se aeftera Geola,* the 'latter' Yule. 'Yule' came from the Old Norse for the heathen feast that lasted twelve days and celebrated not Christmas but the return of the sun.

Wolf-month, Three-milking-month, Storm-felling-month — all are pleasantly evocative. But Cabbage-month! February deserves better than that. Yet even Shakespeare was not very complimentary. 'Good morrow, Benedick,' says Don Pedro in *Much Ado About Nothing;* 'why, what's the matter, That you have such a February face, so full of frost, of storm and cloudiness?'

Yet if ever February failed to live up to its reputation, it came in for criticism. All the weather portents during the month used to be scrutinized earnestly.

'If in February there falls no rain, the hay won't prosper, nor the grain.'

'If the cat in February basks by the gate, in March she will creep into the grate.'

'All the other months of the year, Most heartily curse a fine Februeer.'

*

If any refutation were needed of the image of February as 'Cabbage-month', it is embodied in the Ammil, as it is known on Dartmoor, though the phenomenon can happen anywhere in the right conditions and is sometimes known as a silver-thaw. (It can also occur in March.) It takes place during a severe winter when snow and frost, thaw and rain combine to produce one of the most dramatic and beautiful of natural effects.

As if ice-locked streams and fantastic snowdrifts with their sometimes purple tinges and the magical frost-ferns and filigrees on window-panes are not enough, Nature sets out to surpass herself. A necessary ingredient in her *tour de gobelets* is soft mizzling rain that falls although the temperature above the earth's surface is still well below freezing-point.

Swiftly, as if at the touch of a wand, every gorse bush, hawthorn twig, blade of grass, tussock of heather, dead bracken-frond, sheaf of reeds, every pine-needle, every fence and gate, stone wall, boulder, every single object, is sheathed in delicate ice as if coated in molten crystal that has instantly set. Even the ugliness of barbed wire is transformed and its hurtful spikes are disguised as pearls. A ram's skull is transformed frighteningly, the eye-sockets rimmed with an icy glitter so that it seems like a mask in some nightmare carnival. If the sun then shines, the entire scene becomes a luminous sea of dazzling beauty and the shafts of light sparkle and dance in ten thousand points, each one a wonder in itself.

Above this elf-land the tors brood like phantom glaciers, while the trees in the cleaves and valleys resemble the masts and rigging of doomed ships lost in eternal ice. Only the wind seems alive and every now and then it plucks mischievously at the branches, bringing down a cascade of snowy fragments. Then, as if enjoying its fun, it blows a little harder and an overweighted bough comes crashing down in a jagged explosion like the sound of a giant chandelier falling. Vivid words by Douglas St Leger-Gordon.

But 'majestic though in ruin' as this may be, it is all a terrible beauty, the beauty of death, like something out of a fairy tragedy by Topelius or Hans Andersen. When February is like that, even the rabbits have been known to starve; and if they cannot endure, far less well-equipped for it are the sheep and cattle and ponies that hill-farmers have failed to succour in time.

*

Left undisturbed, ravens will return year after year to the same nesting-site. Even in those places from which the species has vanished, there still exist 'raven trees' in which the birds were once known to nest.

Wood-pigeon shooting of course goes on throughout the winter. But February is the classic month for it, particularly for organized shoots. In arable and wooded areas the air of a Saturday afternoon is punctuated by shot after shot, the dull pop in the distance, the ugly shattering roar close by. The flocks wheel to and fro, kept on the move by the gunners.

In former years some landlords would allow their tenants or farmhands the run of the estate for a day during the month, solely for pigeon-shooting. They would scarcely have done so in the case of pheasant or partridge; besides pigeon-shooting has always been regarded as somewhat of a plebeian sport anyway. In fact, the wood-pigeon (or ring-dove or cushat or cuscott or cullier or queert) is an extremely difficult target. Its thick plumage is proof against anything but a direct hit; it is wary and cunning to a degree. It flies with thrilling speed and has the eyes of a hawk – appropriate enough, for its chief predators in long-lamented days were peregrine falcon, goshawk and sparrowhawk.

Villain though the wood-pigeon may be in the eyes of agriculturalists, it is only because of human activities that it has flourished so prodigiously. In mediaeval times and much later, it was a relatively unknown bird. The fifteenth-century *Book of Saint Albans* has no mention of it among its catalogue of 'swannes and partryches and chekyns'. As late as the 1800s it was so rare in parts of Scotland that the discovery of a nest was a great feat, while people went specially to see a wood-pigeon feeding in a cottage garden during a severe snowstorm.

But then the wood-pigeon population increased dramatically. Originally the wood-pigeon had been a woodland bird, dependent on beechmast, acorns, holly berries. With the development of arable farming in the eighteenth century, the species was provided with ideal nourishment in the form of clover, grain, turnip-tops, peas, brassicas. In the last decade or two it has been expertly calculated that the wood-pigeon population in Britain rises to around ten million after the breeding-season. In a lesser way its descents can remind one of the visitations of locusts. It will strip acre after acre of 'greens', while there are individual cases of more than a thousand grains of wheat being taken from one pigeon's crop and 160 peas from another's.

In this respect Gilbert White records a nice piece of opportunism. 'One of my neighbours shot a ring-dove on an evening as it was returning from feeding and going to roost. When his wife had picked and drawn it, she found the craw stuffed with the most nice and tender tops of turnips. These she washed and boiled and sat down to a choice and delicate plate of greens, culled and provided in this extraordinary manner.' Presumably the good woman enjoyed the pigeon as well. For dry and strong though the flesh may be, properly treated it is fine fare, preferably after hanging for several days.

Pest though the ring-dove is to the farmer, it is a very beautiful bird, with its predominantly blue-grey mantle, vinous breast, patches of iridescent purple and green on the sides of its neck, and a distinctive white collar. Its smoothly ecstatic nuptial display when it rises at a steep angle and then glides down with scarcely open wings, is one of the pleasantest of natural sights. As for its croodling song, for song it must be called, this is redolent of warm leafy days but can still be heard in November, for it is only then that the ring-dove interrupts its strenuous mating. Meredith again:

> *Doves of the fir-wood walling high our red roof*
> *Through the long noon coo, crooning through the coo.*

Traditionally, the song is interpreted as 'Tak' two coos, Taffy, tak' two coos, Taffy, tak' ...' but there is no sharp 'tak' in it and to me it is like 'Don't scold so, Susie, don't scold so, Susie'.

As the blood-red sun sinks enormously behind the leafless woods, the firing rises to a climax, for the birds are trying to roost. Gun in hands, I stand waiting under the drooping canopy of a holly tree. A grey squirrel curses on principle; a blackbird

Farmer and friend: the dog has
overcome his lupine instincts to
become a useful partner in the task
of shepherding. The farm cats in
the background have retained their
independent spirit.

sees ghosts and plunges into a bush to avoid them; a robin whispers chidingly. Hiccuping with alarm a cock pheasant struts uneasily past ten yards away and presently goes rocketing on to a branch. A tawny owl comes and perches almost over my head; he peers and cranes at me uncertainly, then floats off again discreetly.

All round in the spare twilight pigeons are settling in the trees. Fat, chunky birds, sitting targets, they are limned against the sky which is so much lighter than down here in the wood. The first star has appeared, but even now the distant cannonade goes on, though it is diminishing. I break my gun, unship the cartridges and creep away. The pigeons do not stir. If I had tried to stalk them they would have been off in a whipcrack explosion of wings. Out in the lane a farmhand who has taken part in the shoot is tardily fetching his cows. I lurk in the hedgeside dusk until he has gone past, reluctant to meet him and admit that my game-bag is empty. It would be even more difficult to tell him that I hadn't even fired a shot, but had immensely enjoyed the afternoon nonetheless.

*

St Valentine whose feastday is celebrated on 14th February was a Roman priest imprisoned during the third century AD by Claudius II for giving comfort to Christians persecuted for their faith. He compounded his crime by converting his gaoler, the Roman legionary Asterius, whereupon the Emperor caused him to be flogged and subsequently beheaded.

Nobody quite knows the connection between the martyr and the 'valentines', tributes of love and affection, usually tinged with facetiousness ('never sign a walentine with your own name,' counselled Sam Weller), that are exchanged on the day. It has been suggested that St Valentine's Day became mixed up with 15th February, when the heathen festival of Lupercus, the Roman Pan, was celebrated.

Be that as it may, 14th February is also traditionally regarded as the day on which birds mate – 'Saint Valentine is past, Begin these wood birds but to couple now?' But the birds have already begun to fight and court, and ironically, even in a mild winter, the 14th is almost invariably the signal for a cold spell, though this in no wise subdues the flashing wings and eager voices.

Some birds, far from waiting for St Valentine, have long since begun to pair; the earliest of all are the ravens. I have known ravens to start carrying nesting material as early as the first week of the month. As for their nuptial flight, a raven will carry up a stick in its beak, drop it deliberately, and swoop down again to catch it. A pair of birds will soar and roll, corkscrew and dive and turn turtle in wonderful and ecstatic aerial control. On the nest they will pretend to grapple with their beaks, in the so-called 'raven's kiss'.

They possess an extraordinary range of notes and calls,
including an almost goose-like honk, a veritable chuckle, a
houndlike *wuff wuff* that is followed by a rather sotto voce
whistle. Most familiar is the deep, resonant croak of *wuk wuk
wuk* (sometimes rendered as *glog glog*) which on occasions can
be heard when the birds are flying at such great heights that they
are difficult to distinguish visually. In Cornwall this cry used to
be interpreted as 'Corpse, corpse'.

> *There were three ravens sat on a tree,*
> *They were black as black might be.*
> *The one of them said to his mate,*
> *'Where shall we our breakfast take?'*

In contrast, the raven will in courtship utter positively tender
notes, and to listen unseen to a pair of ravens at their nest is to be
enchanted by their caressingly affectionate conversation.

✳

In bygone days when many a countryman kept a pig in a
backyard sty, February was the traditional month for it to be
killed; an 'r' in the month really mattered. Up to about a quarter
of a century ago, when it was made illegal and all pigs had to be
sent to the bacon factory or abattoir, the slaughtering would be

Sheep and cattle were domesticated while Man was still a nomad. The pig had to wait until the establishment of permanent settlements, for it doesn't like forced marches.

done on the home-premises by the itinerant pig-killer. The carcase was then cut up and salted down, while home-cured hams wrapped in muslin and hanging from the beams of farmhouse kitchens were a common and nicely prosperous sight. Nothing was wasted; as they used to say in Cornwall, the only part of the pig you couldn't use was the squeal.

In Hardy's *Jude the Obscure* there is a passage which, allowing for the fact that Jude and Arabella botched the job, exactly describes the procedure for killing a pig which had remained unchanged for centuries and only came to an end in our hygienic days. It was a bloody yet horribly fascinating business, heralded by the lighting of the copper fire in an outhouse. The desperately strong pig knew instinctively that something was amiss even before the men came with ropes to bind him. Alas, the high-pitched porcine squeals of 'Murder!' had no effect except to induce severe hysteria among the poultry. There followed the swift, expert sticking (for you do not *cut* a pig's throat), the reverent collection of the gouting black blood for the manufacture of black pudding, the lashing of the soon defunct pig to a ladder which was then propped upright, the scalding and scraping of the bristles with all the care a barber might show, and

finally the skilled, surgical dissection of that strangely naked, pallid carcase, spreadeagled vertically and upside-down. It looked bizarrely manlike; like someone who had spent all his days shut off from the sunlight. No wonder certain cannibals used to talk of 'long pig'.

As children long ago we would race eagerly to the neighbouring farm at the stirring cry of 'A pig's being killed!'; however, when I came to keep pigs myself I always felt an unhappy pang as the cattle lorry trundled away with another batch peering in bewilderment between the slats. For pigs, old-fashioned pigs that is to say, perhaps not the modern pigs condemned to a twilight life, are extremely likeable characters. They are highly intelligent, exceedingly amiable (except in the case of certain wicked old boars, or sows whose piglings are threatened) and will follow you about like a dog. They have a keen sense of the absurd and will suddenly take off in a collective giddy fit, twirling round and round to the accompaniment of hoarse pantings, guffaws, it might almost be said, of merriment. Perhaps this is when they have caught sight of the wind – for the pig is reputed to be the only animal that can see the wind, as an old farmer once earnestly assured me. And he had certainly never read *Lorna Doone* in which Richard Blackmore makes the same assertion.

As for the pig's reputation for filthiness, this is simply a libel. By nature the pig is as clean as a badger if properly cared for, and a dirty pig is a reflection not on itself but on its owner. Of course pigs revel in a mud-bath but, as with their distant relative the hippopotamus, this is to protect them from the sun, for they have delicate skins.

Their sense of smell is notorious and I used to lose dozens of eggs when the hens laid 'wild' under hedge or bramble-brake, for the sows would invariably snuff the nests out first. But the most remarkable instance of porcine olfactory skill was Slut of New Forest fame. Her owners, the brothers Smith, who lived in Napoleonic times, trained her to point game – pheasant, partridge, rabbit, hare, blackcock – and she was as expert as any gun-dog.

*

It is not only the housewife who practises spring-cleaning. In *The Tale of Mr Tod,* Beatrix Potter, doyenne of nursery stories involving animals, grievously defamed the character of the badger (Tommy Brock to her, other aliases being the Saxon bawson, pate, grey, while badger itself comes from the French *bêcheur,* a digger). She described him as having filthy habits.

This is palpably untrue, for the badger is renowned for its cleanliness. It scrapes its claws against the bark of trees, licks its paws with catlike regularity, searches its young's fur for parasites. Unlike some domestic animals such as the cow which dungs on the spot and often goes around plastered with its own filth, the badger takes great pains to construct a series of latrines at an appreciable distance from its sett.

Miss Potter's natural history was also at fault when she said that Tommy Brock often made use of Mr Tod the fox's various homes. The opposite is true, for it is the fox who takes advantage of the badger's extensive digging. This sometimes causes friction, for the fox has the dangerous habit of leaving tell-tale evidence of his depredations at the entrance to his adopted dwelling.

Moreover, the badger could be called house-proud; not only is he constantly extending and renovating his premises, but he frequently changes his bedding. In autumn he gathers large bundles of dead leaves and bracken, clutching them to his chest as he backs down into the sett. Ernest Neal told me of a badger that helped itself to the straw thatch of a tumbledown shelter that had been constructed by a gamekeeper.

In February a great deal of spring-cleaning takes place and this is often a sign that cubs are present. For while they are confined underground they obviously foul their bedding much more. The sow-badger conscientiously turns out quantities of stale litter that has become mixed with earth and this can sometimes be found in heaps not far from the main entrance. What is more, according to some evidence, badgers will even spring-clean parts of a sett not intended for immediate use and will then go and live somewhere else, leaving the freshly renovated chamber ready for their return later in the year: rather as royalty in ancient times used to go on progresses while a previous residence was being aired and sweetened after its occupation.

March

The Saxons, again according to Verstegan, called March *Lenct-month*. Ash Wednesday is just as likely to fall in February, but as the earliest date on which Easter can fall is 22nd March, clearly most if not all the month is taken up by Lent.

For Christians Lent is a six-week period of fasting, in which abstinence from eating meat is an important feature, leading up to the church's most significant festival, Easter. In fact it is, or was, a convenient way of making a virtue of necessity. For many centuries it was simply impractical to eat meat during the worst and latter part of the winter; there was not enough to go round.

English farming was based on the 'open field' system, and it began to alter in character only through the impetus of periodic 'enclosures' which started in Tudor times and gave, however controversially, progressive landlords the opportunity to farm more intensively. Previously, something like a huge allotment was administered by each village community, the individual peasants, or groups of them, working a number of narrow strips of land, which were not even combined in one workable unit, but were scattered among their neighbours' strips. The strips were not enclosed although at certain crucial times they were flimsily protected by wattle-hurdles to keep out marauding livestock (for the 'typical' English hedge is not always as ancient as is sometimes imagined). After the harvest, all the local farmland would more or less revert to common grazing. And anyone who lives in the country knows what bickerings can arise over that, even today.

This unsatisfactory system meant that the majority of peasants produced only enough to feed their own families and fulfil the demands of their feudal lords — and pay the iniquitous tithes the church demanded. Farming was at a subsistence level: not only was it impossible for the peasants to provide enough meat for the townsfolk, they could not even keep themselves supplied throughout the year. The hay-crop was poor and root-farming was far off in the future, so the bulk of the cattle had to be slaughtered and salted down at the onset of winter. Only the necessary breeding-stock was kept and even this was difficult.

From Christmas to May
Weak cattle decay.

Towards the end of winter, the question of food supplies became acute, so Lent would have had to be invented even if Christianity had not taken hold in the West. It was a sheer economic necessity as was the eating of fish on Fridays during the rest of the year. As late as the reigns of the Tudors and Stuarts attempts were made to enforce Wednesday and Saturday as additional meatless days though this was partly to help the English fisherman who were so essential in manning the Royal Navy. But, like Lent, those 'Fish Days' were necessitated by poor farming. The fishermen of England had to take a big hand in feeding the people.

Only in the eighteenth century, thanks to farming pioneers such as 'Turnip' Townshend, Coke of Norfolk, and Robert Bakewell, did agriculture begin to take on a modern look. In less than seventy years during that epoch the average weight of cattle and sheep sold at Smithfield Market doubled.

✳

In the blustering wind the rooks looked like pieces of burnt paper blown to and fro, jet black against the blue sky as they examined their old nests, helped vocally by the jackdaws which so often accompany them.

The sudden challenging twang of a horn echoed out from the valley road, followed presently by the gritty clip-clop of hooves. At once the rooks abandoned their tentative home repairs and went diving and jinking in cawing curiosity above the hunt as it jogged past, the flag-waving hounds looking so benign one would in due course be startled by their awful baying when they hit a scent.

The rooks were not the only spectators, for the miry, creaking press was followed close at heel ('Hold hard, damn your eyes!') by various nudging motor-cars and Land Rovers; even the postman got out of his van to watch, while legging it along in the rear came an eager stumble of pedestrians cawing in their own fashion as excitedly as the rooks. After a hard winter's curtailment, everyone was eager to get on the trail of blood once more; besides, the end of the season was not all that far off.

Hunting in any form is an emotive subject. Many people regard it with anathema, sometimes violent, though inconsistently stag and hare evoke more sympathy than does the 'red thief'. But in spite of its being a case of the unspeakable in full pursuit of the uneatable, as Oscar Wilde put it, fox-hunting is still part of the English scene, notwithstanding the relentless urbanization that goes on. Indeed, in spite of democracy for in some parts of the country miners are among the keenest fox-hunters. Besides, wasn't the incomparable Jorrocks a grocer?

Yet fox-hunting is not as long-standing as is often imagined. Until the time of Charles I deer-hunting was the gentleman's sport *par excellence*. It was the Civil War which in so many

Primitive Man did not hunt for sport. He killed only to feed and clothe himself. Not until after Man had domesticated certain animals for food supplies and other reasons did he take to hunting wild animals for recreation.

matters caused a social revolution. Many of the great estates were broken up or confiscated, deer-parks were abandoned or plundered, many of the deer were killed by roving soldiery. So at the Restoration, as gentlemen positively have to hunt *something*, they took to chasing the fox.

Even so, as late as Victoria's reign, there were one-third more packs of harriers than packs of fox-hounds. But fox-hunting kept gaining ground in the popular imagination, with its dramatic cross-country gallops, thrusting squireens and half-pay captains crashing over hedges, with the frequent bonus for onlookers of a spectacular fall, the so-called music of the hounds, the blaring horn and the scarlet coats. A whole literature grew up around it, from the roaring pot-house songs such as *D'ye ken John Peel* to the novels of R. S. Surtees and his inimitable characters including James Pigg, the Geordie huntsman, who opined that 'there's *nout* like huntin', to which his master John Jorrocks of Great Coram Street responded 'Dash my vig! So say I! So say I! It's the real Daffy's Elixir! The Cordial Balm o' Gilead! The concentrated Essence of Joy!'

As somebody once remarked, it would be interesting to hear the fox's reaction.

In addition, the frog is much livelier in its movements and has considerable leaping powers. The toad can take a very short reluctant jump, but mostly crawls ponderously about his affairs and bears no resemblance to that boastful road-hog who went poop-poop-poop as he raced along in *The Wind in the Willows*.

But the toad can on occasions, especially if it is being menaced by a grass snake, one of its predators, present a formidable appearance. It will inflate its body to a grotesque size while at the same time raising itself stiff-legged at the full stretch of its limbs. Presumably all this is to make it impossible for the snake to seize hold of it.

As for Shakespeare's 'ugly and venomous toad' which 'wears yet a precious jewel in his head', the glands behind the eyes do produce a bitter, offensive fluid though this cannot really be called a poison. And the jewel in its head must surely be a reference to its beautiful eyes which are a bright, coppery red.

*

In the distance the tractors, red, blue, yellow, look like Dinky toys as they crawl down the huge field, the illusion heightened by the silence, for the wind is in the wrong direction and they cannot be heard. The ploughshares gouge into the green turf, exposing glistening muscles of upturned soil which, you feel, might well be writhing in agony as the machines relentlessly munch their way onward. In their wake float pearly white sea-gulls and nicely contrasting black rooks, waiting to pounce on those sinews of the earth.

Slowly through the day the field will be transformed as the gigantic pattern of furrows is stitched over it. But the tractors, some people would say, are ploughing the wrong way. They ought to be working across the slope, the better to avoid erosion which the downward ploughing is more likely to induce – though others would say this does not allow the water to drain away.

All too rarely, it seems these days, do we enjoy the proverbial peck of March dust that is worth a king's ransom. But when March is like that there is an atavistic satisfaction in watching the ploughs at work in the spring sunshine, with the first dandelions like tiny shards of the sun's light and brimstone butterflies like much paler flakes. For the plough, above all else, was instrumental in Man's transition from hunter to settled farmer.

Even when Stone Age Man began to domesticate cattle and sheep he continued to lead a nomadic existence; then, taking his cue from nature, he started to grow crops of a meagre kind. But he was still a nomadic pastoralist. For with his primitive tools – perhaps a deer's antler or a stick with a stone head attached – he could do little more than scratch the surface of the soil. In any case much of Britain and Europe was covered with forest, against which flint instruments were of little use. So he tilled his modest crops for a season until the soil of that particular area was

At times snipe consort in small parties called wisps – one of those pleasant collective nouns catalogued in Dame Juliana Berner's *The Boke of Saint Albans* – such as a charm of goldfinches, an exaltation of larks, an unkindness of ravens.

exhausted, then he moved on with his herds to start his semi-nomadic life all over again.

Bronze was certainly a great improvement over flint. But by far the biggest step forward in Man's progress was the discovery of the way to make iron. It was iron that enabled Man to take seriously to settled farming. The first true farmers in Britain were the Celts who crossed over from Europe some three thousand years ago. But far more effective were the Belgae who followed them a thousand years later – a generation or two before the start of the Christian era. The Belgae were skilled ironmasters and smiths and they introduced a revolutionary iron-shod plough of a comparatively advanced design. The Belgic plough, forerunner of the modern implement with its coulter and mouldboard, and drawn by oxen, changed the face of the land – and also Man's history.

It was from this time that, however slowly, agriculture began to come into its own, and Man had the chance of producing more food than he needed for his own dependents. Until there was such a surplus there could be no urban life. So the ploughman, dismissed by many people as a rustic figure wearily plodding his homeward way at the tolling of the curfew, is in effect an important historic character, the builder of cities from which, for better or worse, stemmed so much of our civilization, our arts, sciences and skills. And the young men in their tractor-cabs, listening to their transistors, represent an unbroken line from the far-off days when that mythical but symbolic Tubal Cain 'fashioned the first ploughshare'.

But I didn't say that to them when we had a pint at the local later. They would have given me a very odd look. We talked about the Grand National instead.

✳

For me at least, largely because I associate it with my boyhood, one of the most nostalgic of spring sounds is the drumming of the snipe. I still remember the very first time I heard one, on a farm near the Beaulieu River, the unlikely tenant of which had migrated from the faraway Isle of Bute. As I picked my way through bogland, thick with phalanxes of flags and clumps of sweet-gale whose fragrant catkins were already burgeoning, I heard a goat bleating, sometimes quite clearly, sometimes apparently much farther off. Most mystifying of all, the noise came from high up in the sky. It was rather disturbing; I felt quite uneasy, as if some strange unearthly creature was abroad.

It was of course no goat, but a snipe 'drumming' overhead. Later on I found it was not so foolish to liken it to the bleating of a goat, for in parts of the country, especially the northern moors, the snipe is called the Heather-bleater, while the Gaelic name for it is *Gobhair-adhair*, the Goat-of-the-Air.

Until the turn of the century there was much controversy

about how exactly the snipe makes this characteristic sound. Charles St John for instance took it for granted that it was simply a peculiar cry, and earlier still Gilbert White wrote that 'In breeding-time snipes play over the moor, piping and humming: they always hum as they are descending. Is not their hum ventriloquious like that of the turkey?'

But, significantly, the author of *The Natural History of Selborne* went on to remark: 'Some suspect that it is made by their wings.'

And that, of course, is nearer the case. The snipe rises high and fast in towering circles, then makes a series of sudden slanting descents with wings half closed and tail spread. Most important of all, the outer feathers of the tail are held stiffly at right angles. It is the rushing of air through these feathers as the snipe dives repeatedly and steeply that causes the distinctive sound (rather like the effect of an arrow), the intervals of silence occur when the bird rises up again before flinging itself headlong and ecstatically earthward once more, for the benefit of its mate who sits brooding her darkly blotched eggs where, as John Clare wrote,

> *The trembling grass*
> *Quakes from the human foot*
> *Nor bears the weight of man to let him pass.*

*

If one wished to nominate an 'animal of the month', it would in March undoubtedly be the hare. For it is late in the month (and in early April) that the Mad March Hare truly lives up to its nickname. The hare is not always the timid figure often portrayed ('the hare limped trembling through the frozen grass'). Driven by the mating-urge it is transformed into a zany character seized, if it can be so expressed, by a ferocious vertigo.

One pair of males I watched opened their almost eyeball-to-eyeball encounter by confronting each other for a long time without moving, perhaps sizing up the situation. Then abruptly one of them made at the other, leapt clean over him and let loose a double kick with his hind legs that caught his rival a thump in the ribs.

This they considered with the deliberation of a Karpov and a Korchnoi; then the second hare leapt in his turn and bucked, paff, paff! with equal savagery. He landed close to the other and, sitting on their hunkers, they boxed, dabbing muzzles but doing no damage. Their respective corners were held by several other hares which had loped closer, some of them looking like bicyclists as they humpled hugely on the skyline.

After that breather the serious part of the bout was resumed. It was a mad, ludicrous display that worked up to a crescendo, which might almost be called ecstasy, but for the fact that under

the apparently lunatic behaviour there was something savage, for they put all the strength of their tawny bodies into each kick. You felt they really wanted to hurt each other, and this evidently happened, for after they had skedaddled and pranced and leapt, one of them cried enough and went crippling away toward a hawthorn thicket. However, the other had tasted victory and cantered after him, whereupon the quitter, desperate, vaulted over him and dealt him a blow on the head that made him huddle as if stunned, which maybe he was.

It has been known for a pursuing stoat to be bowled over by those immensely powerful hind legs, and the eighteenth-century poet William Cowper, writing in *The Gentleman's Magazine* about his pet hares, describes how after supper he always admitted them into the parlour.

> *One evening the cat, being in the room, had the hardiness to pat Bess [one of the hares] upon the cheek, an indignity which he resented by drumming upon her back with such violence that the cat was happy to escape from under his paws, and hide herself.*

Those long legs enable the hare to swim well when necessary and to cover the ground fast and far, though they can be a handicap when it travels downhill – if you watch a hare descending you will find it usually does so diagonally across the contours. And they earned the hare some of its ancient names, such as Big Bum and Old Turpin the fast traveller. Equally important to the hare's defence, however, is its eyesight. Its prominent eyes are so situated that it can look behind as efficiently as it can look to the front giving virtually all-round vision.

March is the traditional mating-time of the hare, although its breeding season goes on during many months of the year. The mating-urge transforms the usually timid hare into a ferocious character as can be seen in this photograph of two males that have just broken off their conflict.

The mole is marvellously adapted for its underground life. Its rigid, splayed forepaws allow it almost to 'swim' through the earth. Its cylindrical body exactly fits its tunnels; its velvety coat brushes both forwards and backwards.

murmur on which is borne the ineffable scent of re-awakening life – for this is sometimes still apparent in spite of the various effluvia that charge the air.

When this happens it is as if a curtain had been raised. All at once the 'Lent lilies', those small delightful wild daffodils are thronging the river bank, and though not a Wordsworth fan, I too 'gazed – and gazed'. In the lane the blackthorn's snowy stars adorn the spiky black leafless twigs and on the banks the windflower nods to the wild strawberry flowers.

The chiff-chaff is often regarded as the earliest migrant, but glad though I always am to hear that demure *chiff chiff chiff* (it's never *chiff chaff*), the wheatear is my first venturer from overseas. His white rump – which gives him his name, for the word wheatear comes from the Old English white arse – is unmistakable as he flits pertly from rock to rock, uttering his warning cry that sounds like stones being struck together, appropriate enough in his moorland haunts. But this smart, handsome bird is not nearly as numerous as it used to be. In the last century it used to be extensively trapped with horsehair snares set in little tunnels and was sold in large numbers to restaurants for the delectation of Victorian gourmands; at the same time poulterers' shops used to be adorned with skylarks.

One of the most surprising aspects of this 'spring rush' that is now developing all round us, is the ferocity of the mole towards his rivals. Usually this velvety engineer leads a solitary life, but at breeding-time the males or boars fight savage battles and a dead animal I found had probably starved to death as a result of being constantly chased above ground and prevented from appeasing its voracious appetite.

April

Mr Maddowcroft is still lambing — we are always later in these parts. His flock is not big enough to warrant a full-time shepherd, so he does the work himself and the ewes are mainly in the home field, near at hand for his nightly rounds. He complains bitterly that recently he has lost three newborn lambs. 'Them dratted foxes, they make me feel real wicked.'

'Wicked' in our vocabulary is angry, and he certainly is that. But he listens politely to my oft-repeated assertion that there are too many dogs around and he knows full well that some of them go sheeping. I know for a fact that last year he himself shot an Alsatian. It is also a fact that many a farmer, especially near certain towns, has given up keeping sheep because of the trouble he has had with uncontrolled dogs.

Undoubtedly foxes do take the occasional lamb; but undoubtedly, too, when they are skulking in the neighbourhood of lambing ewes they are often merely in search of the afterbirth. Undoubtedly again, though it is hard work convincing farmers such as my neighbour, dogs do much of the damage foxes are blamed for.

I cannot help thinking that there must be some significance in the reaction of various farm animals to foxes and dogs respectively. Time after time, in broad daylight, I have seen a fox stroll across a field without the sheep, even those with lambs, taking the slightest notice. I have seen the same thing with pigs and cattle. But let a dog appear on the horizon and the sheep go huddling off in panic.

Cattle that scarcely give a glance at a fox stand no nonsense from dogs and one of the rare occasions when Laska my labrador is daunted is on encountering them, especially aggressive Galloways down from the moor. With hackles raised and eyes rolling, she will make a wide detour to avoid them, taking refuge on some convenient bank if possible. As for pigs and dogs, the most spectacular incident I ever saw was when my own sows routed the local hunt.

At the time I had twelve sows and gilts, all in pig. One morning we heard the baying of the pack not far away and went out to watch. The sows were grazing over a wide area, some of them a furlong apart. A few couple of hounds came over the steep bank into the field, trying to unravel the scent. Susie, the doyenne of the little herd, pricked up her ears and watched. The other sows stopped grazing, too. The rest of the pack streamed after their companions and whimpering and baying they ran down the field parallel to the drove from which they had come.

This was too much for Susie. Her first questioning grunts which had alerted the herd now changed to a savage, warlike utterance, the like of which I had never heard. It was chilling in its intensity. It was taken up by the other sows who now began to close rapidly on their chieftainess, with whom, almost shoulder to shoulder, they charged at the intruders. That squadron of sows charged for nearly a hundred yards and, in spite of the scent, those twenty-six couple of hounds stayed not upon the order of their going, but went, scrambling with utter indignity through the brambles and holly bushes that topped the bank.

It was all the more spectacular because it was an invitation meet and the lane was crowded with an astonished field.

*

Every so often reports appear in local newspapers about mysterious, nocturnal, seemingly phantom attacks on people homeward bound along country lanes. All a person thus assaulted is aware of is a startling buffet on the head. I was reminded of this by a neighbour complaining that his son had been thus assailed. Near the same place a year ago I had been similarly attacked.

The culprits could be heard and occasionally seen night after night. They were a pair of tawny owls who had their young ones in a hollow oak-tree close by. I knew the nest well enough but was chary of investigating too closely, being acquainted with the pugnacity of tawny owls at rearing time.

The late T. A. Coward (whose bird books I was brought up on) wrote that 'a Tawny with young will strike a man with its claws on the head or neck, though it will not attack his face.' The answer to the latter part of his observation is not to tell it to the Marines, but rather to Eric Hosking. It was while photographing young tawny owls that he was attacked by a parent bird and lost an eye as a result – which at least provided him with a title for his autobiography: *An Eye for a Bird*.

But in daylight the owl is lost: not long before those particular birds started nesting a hideous avian cacophony was going on one morning as I went into the garden. The barking of crows, rattling of magpies, counterpoint of jackdaws, *chink chink chink* of blackbirds, assorted piping of finches, wrens, robins, made it obvious what was happening. The for-once unfriendly neighbourhood birds had waylaid a tawny owl returning home late and were mobbing it hysterically, the small birds especially wreaking vengeance for all the terrors of the night.

The owl sat close up by the trunk of the tree, eyes closed against the morning sun.

*

In the April sunshine a viper lay basking in a damp hollow, almost artificially surrounded by primroses as if it had chosen the spot purposely to set off its beauty. It was enjoying the combination of warmth and moistness and was reluctant to move. It lay there gleaming a handsome dark red-brown, so dark in fact that the central wavy black line was scarcely visible, though on its sides a series of whitish oval spots stood out. Presently, after an admonitory hiss, its forked tongue flickering, it glided slowly away. It was not very long, perhaps eighteen inches, and was probably a male, for the female viper is usually longer.

Much as one admires the beauty of the snake and marvels at this strange, mysterious creation, it is difficult to suppress the thrill of apprehension that it evokes. Yet the danger in this country from our only venomous snake, the viper, is greatly exaggerated. Any snake is always more anxious to avoid human presence than to attack. Snakebites happen by accident when the snake has not had time to get out of the way; the snake is deaf and depends for its 'hearing' on the tremors of the ground. Very few people in normal health die from a viper's bite in Britain. There are still those who are under the impression that it is the snake's tongue through which the venom passes, but it is of course the hinged fangs which channel it. The tongue is the snake's most important olfactory organ with which it 'tastes' the air.

Some people, too, imagine that all snakes are automatically poisonous and the harmless grass snake often suffers because of this. In fact the two species can be distinguished by a number of characteristics. Generally speaking, the viper is dark coloured – it can be quite black occasionally – usually, but not always, with a zigzag stripe along the back and an inverted V or an X behind the head. Its jaws are much more prominent, the head showing up more distinctively than in the grass snake where there is an absence of a defined neck. In colour the grass snake is usually olive green with a characteristic yellow patch on either side of the neck. Again, the pupil of its eye is round, like that of the smooth snake, not slitlike as in the viper. The grass snake is much longer and more graceful than the thickset viper. When frightened or captured, the grass snake emits a fetid stink. Gilbert White tells of one captive that 'filled the room with such nauseous effluvia as rendered it hardly supportable.'

The third snake that exists in Britain, the smooth snake or coronella, is now so rare that it is a protected species, existing only in certain sandy, heathy regions of southern England. I have only once set eyes on one.

Later the same morning I caught sight of what at first appeared to be another snake, quite immobile. It was in fact a snake-skin recently sloughed and could have belonged to the viper I had seen earlier. Throughout its life, a snake sloughs or moults its skin doing this three or four times a year as it grows. First, the skin starts to split and loosen along the jaws and the

The viper possesses hinged poison fangs which lie flat when the mouth is closed. The venom is pumped out under pressure through an enclosed duct, the effect being like that of a hypodermic needle.

snake in effect crawls out of it, helping the process by fraying the old skin on any handy object. When first sloughed, the skin closely retains the form of the snake, and I had to glance a second time before realizing what this one was.

✳

As I walked along the riverbank a slim, dark brown animal came bounding and rippling down the slope at right angles some twenty yards away. It must have been nearly eighteen inches in length and looked at first like a huge stoat. But I knew at once that it was a mink. I froze in the shelter of a clump of willows and the mink did not see me. It was too preoccupied following the trail of its prey, for it was quite evidently in full cry.

With all the nimble intensity of the Mustelid family, it went snaking and weaving in and out of the low-draping bushes, remnants of bracken and tussocks of heather. For a moment it seemed as if it had lost the scent. It paused absolutely still, with a forepaw slightly raised as if commanding silence. Gradually its head thrust forward with an alert, menacing manner. Then suddenly it plunged straight into the undergrowth. There followed a brief, violent thrashing punctuated by a squeal that was quickly muffled.

Eager to see more of this drama I walked cautiously nearer. But the mink and its prey, almost certainly a young rabbit, had

vanished. The ground beyond the patch of undergrowth was bare, yet nowhere could I find any trace of them. However, there is little doubt that some time sooner or later that mink and the family it may well be rearing will show up again.

The mink has now become an established feral type in Britain. It was originally imported for breeding on fur-farms. But the mink is an expert escapologist, while many of the people who tried their hand at mink-farming after the war were inexperienced and gave up after a year or two; in the meantime a number of escapes occurred: many in Devonshire, but also in the New Forest, Sussex, Yorkshire, Scotland and elsewhere. In some areas otterhounds are being used to hunt the mink.

One hesitates to apply emotive terms such as ruthless or ferocious to any animal, but they are applicable to the mink. It is among the few animals which kill for the sake of killing. Rabbits, water-voles, fish, wild ducklings, nothing is safe from it. Its great speciality is raiding poultry runs; though occasionally its gluttony leads to its downfall. One noontide a friend of mine in Cornwall walked down to his henyard near the River Inney. It was soon evident that a marauder had been at work. And inside an open laying-hut, sleeping off its repast, lay a mink, curled up snugly. It was so gorged that my friend was able without disturbing it to return to his house two hundred yards away, fetch his shotgun, and walk back again to the henyard. That mink did not wake up, ever.

*O fairest flower, no sooner
    blown but blasted,
Soft silken primrose fading
    timelessly*

– thus Milton; but, perhaps you prefer Beaumont and Fletcher?

*Primrose, first born child of Ver,
Merry Spring-time's harbinger,*

Although the establishment of the mink as a feral species in Britain is due to escapes the effect has been as disastrous as if it had been deliberately introduced.

After watching the mink hunting, I walked on, and as it happened another alien made an appearance. A peevish nattering went on overhead and a grey squirrel went acrobatting along a branch, hardly pausing to judge the distance before vaulting into another tree. This is perhaps the most notorious alien species to have been introduced artificially into Britain. Like the mink, it is a native of North America and was first imported in the 1830s, with a much more serious introduction around 1880. Yet as recently as sixty years ago a naturalist such as Edward Step could write 'In some places in the London district a light grey squirrel may be seen, and thought to be a colour variation of our native species. It is really an American visitor. . .'

Some visitor! It rapidly became established and a population explosion took place. The grey did not actually physically oust the native red squirrel; the latter had already begun to decline, largely through disease, in regions which the grey had not yet penetrated. Subsequently, however, the greater adaptability and fertility of the grey squirrel did affect the native animal, for the American variety has spread rapidly over most of Britain.

The popular image of the squirrel is of a pretty bushy-tailed animal holding a nut in its forepaws. In fact it is virtually omnivorous; as well as hazel-nuts and sweet chestnuts, seeds of many trees, bulbs, roots, catkins, toadstools, garden peas, fruit, insects and grubs all feature in its diet. (Last year grey squirrels devastated my broad beans.) It will take birds' eggs and even fledgelings, while it is anathema to the forester because of its bark-stripping proclivities which often kill young trees.

Many official campaigns have been mounted against it including bounties and cheap cartridges, but without success. The Forestry Commission had to hold a press conference to explain or excuse its use of Warfarin in its struggle against the grey

Little owl fledgelings looking out from their nest hole. Although the species was introduced artificially, it is, as Richard Fitter has said, a British bird manqué, for it would long ago have been a member of our avifauna if only it had spread northwards after the Ice Age before the ancient land bridge between Britain and continental Europe disappeared.

squirrel. Perhaps if the grey squirrel were regarded as a game animal and considered good to eat, as in America, the result might have been different.

That morning's parade of alien species did not end there. A bird, perhaps the size of a song-thrush but with a flatter head and a more compact shape, went floating away erratically through the trees. If I had not recognized it by its 'jizz', as they say, its identity was confirmed by its almost catlike mewing. It was a little owl. This eight or nine-inch bird has perhaps a more distinguished history than mink or grey squirrel, for in classical Greece it was the bird of Pallas Athene and its image appeared on many Greek coins.

Most owls are nocturnal in their habits. The little owl, however, hunts chiefly by day, though it operates at night as well. For a long time it was regarded with great hostility by the automatically prejudiced and often ignorant game-interests, being accused of dire crimes such as lifting pheasant and

partridge chicks. So, forty-odd years ago, the British Trust for Ornithology undertook an exhaustive study of the bird's feeding habits. Nearly 2500 of its pellets were examined and showed conclusively that, like all the owls, the little owl did far more good than harm, for its food consists of rats, mice, other rodents, many noxious insects, worms, frogs and the occasional wild bird, mainly starling and house-sparrow.

In origin the little owl is a native of southern and central Europe, also of Africa and Asia. It was that great if eccentric naturalist Charles Waterton who first introduced the species to Britain in 1843. He purchased a dozen 'Civetta or Little Italian owls' at a market in Rome and released them at Walton Hall, his Yorkshire estate. His attempt failed, but several other naturalists such as Lord Lilford were successful a generation later. Many of the little owls they turned loose had been bought at Leadenhall Market where they were sold by Dutch birdcatchers.

Nowadays you can hear that strange mewing cry almost anywhere in Britain.

*

Every year a pair of missel-thrushes nest somewhere in the garden. They are magnificent birds with their subdued but exceedingly handsome colours, ashy brown mantle and prominently spotted buff-white underparts. Their straightforward purposeful flight and proud, upright stance when at rest add to their impressiveness. The cockbird's song is a defiance in itself.

A party of missel-thrushes at a drinking pool. Later in the year, in August or September, they flock considerably and I have seen gatherings of perhaps eighty birds. The species is partially migratory, some birds wintering in Southern Europe and North Africa.

Once upon a time the scientific name for the cuckoo-pint was *Arum summis labris degustantes mutos redens* 'the arum which strikes dumb those who do but taste it'. It is much simpler to use its aliases, lords-and-ladies or the Devil's men and women.

But they *will* nest in such vulnerable places. Last year they built in an old apple tree which leans wearily nearer the ground with every passing season and is easily accessible to nocturnal feline prowlers. This year the thrushes built in a Norwegian spruce close to the house. To and fro they fly between field and tree, carrying immense beakfuls of wool that look like bizarre moustaches. Sometimes a bird will perch for two or three minutes in full view on post or branch, indifferent to who is watching this obvious activity.

In addition to this habit of building in exposed sites, the missel-thrushes compound their difficulties by being very aggressive and thus drawing attention to themselves. Not for nothing was the missel-thrush nicknamed 'butcher-boy of the woods'. With churring screams and fierce croaks it will mob any trespassing cat and has been known to strike a human being.

The magpie, like other members of the corvine family, is a carrion-eater.

Its worst enemies are magpies (of course that goes for many birds!). While our pair was still building, a spectacular battle took place between them and a couple of sneak-thief magpies doing a recce. It went on partly on the ground, partly in mid-air, in a strident, frantic mêlée that persisted over perhaps a quarter of an hour, for it kept being renewed. But though on that occasion the magpies were driven off, they returned choosing a more profitable time – when the purple-speckled browny white eggs had hatched and there were two fledgelings being fed.

One morning, soon after first light, I was awoken by a truly startling cacophony of bird cries. The harsh screams of the missel-thrushes and the determined rattling of magpies, determined to press home their blatant robbery whatever the opposition: the air was charged with fury and desperation. I threw on some clothes and slip-slopped out to the rescue; too late. Feathers still floated in the air; most omnious of all, very noticeable patches of blood stained the flagstones underneath the tree. In spite of all the efforts of the thrushes the magpies had made off with both the fledgelings. In the distance the thrushes still churred, though disconsolately now, while from the nest dangled wool and moss, dragged out during the struggle.

On all sides now urgent wings pass to and fro as the birds go about their nest-building and there seems less song now than there will be again for a while when the hen-birds are sitting. Nothing illustrates better the infinite variety of nature than the vastly different methods adopted by different birds. Some species, such as magpies, nest in the same tall tree-top site more than one year running. They merely add more sticks to the framework of the old nest, equipping it with a side entrance and covering it with a domed roof; the nest becomes immense at times. The ring-dove takes very little trouble, simply making a platform of twigs with no other nesting material and I have sometimes seen the white eggs from underneath.

The nightjar makes no nest at all, just lays her mottled eggs on the ground; the pheasant at least puts together leaves and grass in a convenient hollow. And under hedgerow or bush the partridge uses similar materials with which she covers her eggs when she quits the nest for a while. The skylark will sometimes make its nest in the hoof-mark of a cow. Like John Clare, 'I have often wondered how birds' nests escape injuries which are built upon the ground' – and why they are not more vulnerable to predatory mammals. Does their scent diminish protectively?

One of the most elaborate nests is made by the long-tailed tit; indeed, it is one of the most beautiful and probably takes a pair of birds a fortnight to build. Oval in shape, perhaps five inches long, it is a masterpiece of weaving, in which moss, wool, lichen, even spider's silk are used – and of course feathers. The bird is aptly nicknamed the 'Feather-poke'. Richard Kearton once counted more than two thousand feathers in one nest he examined. This compact, domed nest is all the more remarkable because a dozen fledgelings – and their mother – crowd into it, while the male bird frequently roosts in it, too.

A bird well known for its nesting habits is the wren. This avian midget, whose scientific name of *Troglodytes troglodytes* is almost as long as itself, originated in North America, whence it found its way to Siberia and subsequently into western Europe. It is an indomitable little bird and always has its tail up, as if to help it balance during its explosive song. The male has a strange penchant for nest-building – 'cock-nests' as they used to be called. Many are never completed, others left unlined. Often the wren's real nest is built in weird places. One was found in a cabbage-top; another, for long kept in Chester Museum, was tucked between the limp wing and dry carcase of a sparrowhawk hanging on a gamekeeper's gibbet.

You can learn a lot about birds' nests in winter. As Edward Thomas put it:

The summer nests uncovered by autumn wind,
Some torn, others dislodged, all dark,
Everyone sees them: low or high in tree,
Or hedge, or single bush, they hang like a mark.

Since there's no need of eyes to see them with
I cannot help a little shame
That I missed most, even at eye's level, till
The leaves blew off and made the seeing no game.

*

Nest-building is not, however, confined to birds. Of all the small boys who have triumphantly carried home jam-jars full of sticklebacks (many of which have subsequently died through lack of oxygen) probably few have realized that this tiny fish is a keen nest-builder. I know I did not until long afterwards.

Sometimes I go down to the cleave early in the morning to wait for a heron which has a regular beat on the river. Over he comes on vast, majestic, deceptively ponderous vans, lanky legs stretched out behind him, long neck curved back, craning round as he carefully reconnoitres the water. The least doubt and away he veers, going with deliberate, powerful strokes over the moor to some other fishing-ground.

He does so this morning, not because he has spotted me, but to escape a gang of foraging rooks which had been making their way back to the rookery in the village churchyard half a mile away. Like a swarm of enormous bees they come mobbing the heron, and the air is shattered by their raucous, bullying shouts.

The heron swerves and swerves again to avoid them. But still they hang on, crowding about him on all sides in corvine hysteria. Over the river they come and rise higher still. Then, abruptly, teetering round in mid-air, the heron drops straight through his pursuers and lands with a tremendous thrashing of wings and branches in a willow tree.

And there he stays, doggedly if awkwardly, while the rooks flutter round, clumsily trying to hover, cawing and sneering at him for a lanky-legged booby, and brushing so close that more than once he has an anxious time keeping his balance. Presently the tumult subsides, and the marauders concentrate on trying to barge the heron from his perch; they fail. The 'crane', to give it its local name, stays there, bolt upright, moving his head now and then, as if to let the rooks observe the sharpness of his long spear of a bill, though he makes no attempt to use it.

This strange enmity between rooks and herons is of long standing. Perhaps it stems from days when herons were far more numerous than they are today and there was more competition for suitable nesting-sites. It was always the rooks, being more numerous and aggressive, who were the offenders and sometimes the skirmishes developed into fierce battles in which both rooks and herons were killed. The constant persecution occasionally resulted in the herons abandoning their colony and setting up elsewhere. But in a few isolated cases the opposite happened. The exasperated herons, finding that passive resistance was useless, took the law into their own hands and successfully expelled the rooks: and then, adding insult to injury, used some of the rook nests as foundations for their own bulky homes.

However, as well as this competition for favourable nesting-sites, could it be that the rooks discovered the herons were a soft touch? Very often the rooks would sally forth and mob herons that were returning with fish for their young, forcing the unfortunate birds to disgorge their burden – and the rooks would proceed to squabble over a free meal. That thieving ploy is well known to others; I have seen a lesser black-backed gull harry a squawking heron until it spewed out its catch, which the gull then retrieved.

May

***

Recently I went deer-stalking. Not, however, on some lordly highland estate, the sort of place where William Scrope and Charles St John indulged their passion, as do their spiritual descendants today. Here is Scrope on the subject of deer-stalking: 'In the pursuit, the stag's motions are so noble, and his reasoning so acute, that, believe me, I had rather follow one hart from morning till night with the expectation of getting a shot, than have the best day's sport with the moorfowl (grouse) that the hills could afford me.' And here is St John: 'There had been seen and reported to me, a particularly large and fine antlered stag, whose branching honours I wished to transfer from the mountain side to the walls of my hall.'

The 'finer' and 'nobler' the animal, the more such sportsmen yearned to kill it! But that is a digression. My deer-stalking was on the Quantock Hills where I had gone for a few days to one of my erstwhile haunts. I was in luck, for during the morning, moving with the patience and caution that must become second nature if you want to have the chance of watching wildlife, I got close to a little herd of nine deer. Forty yards away in a little combe I made out three 'warrantables' antlers already cast, three 'staggards', four-year-olds which keep their antlers longer, and three calves, 'spayads' of about three years.

Elated by good fortune, for I had stumbled on them quite by chance, I sank cautiously on my hunkers, afraid they would melt away all too soon. But I was the right side of the wind, and, like most wild animals, the red deer depends far more on its sense of smell than on sight. But hawthorns obscured my view, so I crawled up the slope, treacherous with dead bracken bents among the whortleberry plants. Nine heads went up; nine pairs of eyes stared. I froze. A stag barked a short, dry, peremptory sound, half roar, half cough. Silence settled on the combe, as if to help the deer discover the intruder.

Presently, reassured, the little herd moved casually to the left. I heard them ranging along about twenty yards away, pulling at the tender leaves. Then I heard a dry clattering, antlers against antlers, and while I lay peering beneath the trees, two staggards came in view. Heads down, muzzles almost touching the ground, they pushed and fenced and clashed their antlers together strenuously. Obviously these, in the process of decay, were irritating them; the deer were trying to hasten the course of greater than is generally realized because of its secretive habits. According to an ancient belief in Scotland, these games took place round a 'spaning-tree' ('spane' meaning to wean) when the doe wanted to distract her young one when the time came for it to be weaned; in fact they are courting-games. A reliable clue to the presence of roe-deer, even without sighting the animals, is the so-called fairy rings round which during the (August) rut the buck chases the doe interminably until well-worn circles are left.

*

In my part of the country there never were many elms. The nearest of any note were in the close of Exeter Cathedral. All had to be felled because of Dutch Elm disease and the place looked singularly naked for a while. But farther 'up country', as they say, one is always, still, saddened by the devastation wrought by the insignificant fungus with the formidable name, *Ceratocystis ulmi*. Transported to its fell task by the large European bark-beetle, *Scolytus scolytus*, it gets into the tree's blood vessels and chokes it to death.

Once upon a time high hopes of saving the elms were placed on the injection under pressure into the vascular system of the trees of fungicides such as Benomyl. At the same time the beetle-carrier was attacked by insecticides sprayed by helicopter. But all this proved far too expensive, according to present-day priorities and Tennyson's 'immemorial elm' has been abandoned to its fate.

Many of the dead trees remain, stark relics of what was for so long such an impressive feature of the English landscape. They stand like disturbing surrealistic presences, as if darkly reminding us of all that is happening to the world of nature around us. Sometimes these dead elms keep company with cornfields on which the stubble has been burned and all around appears devastated as if by warfare.

Perhaps, even though they are not felled, these dead elms will come crashing down in the course of time when their unreliable roots can no longer withstand the gales of winter. Because of its propensity for thus crashing down in high winds and causing accidents, the tree gave rise to the country saying 'Ellum hateth Man, and waiteth'. It is fitting therefore that one of the continuing uses for elm-wood is the making of coffins. In fact it is used for this because of its resistance to decay. For this reason, too, water-mains were once made of bored elm-wood the lengths being joined by iron collars. Some of these water-mains dating from Roman times have been unearthed beneath the Bank of England and can be seen in the London Museum.

One aspect of these stricken elms intrigues me. Very often rookeries were built in the living trees, and even after the visitation of the disease the rooks have kept up their residence and their nests stand out in the naked branches. Now, occasion-

(ABOVE) The Eurasian otter *(Lutra barang)* on the left and the European otter *(L. lutra)* on the right. Otters do a great deal of good by killing sickly fish and also by killing many eels, which are themselves the worst enemies of young fry.

(LEFT) A rookery. Many farmers swear by the rook; others continue to swear at it. One rook's stomach may be stuffed with grain; another one's may be packed with wireworms.

ally in May the sun is hot enough to cause considerable scorching especially high up in an exposed position, and particularly in the case of scantily-clad nestlings. Will the rooks one day come to and realize that something is amiss? So far they have not and the 'clanging' rookery still fight, mate, squabble and rear their young in the forever leafless trees.

✳

I do not know the origin of the expression 'to get one's goat', meaning to irk, annoy or anger. But I have just found it singularly appropriate. We returned home after a weekend away to find obvious signs of caprine depredations. Broad beans eaten down to the ground, albertine stems nibbled off, hydrangeas defoliated; the raiders had even climbed into an appletree with a sloping trunk. More damage was apparent every time we did the rounds of the garden.

The criminals were sedately grazing on the other side of the cart-track lane, cocking insolent yellow eyes at us, wagging their beards gloatingly, in short positively sneering at us, I swear. Struggling with my blood pressure I confronted their owner who, from the erstwhile comfortable old countrywoman I had hitherto taken her to be, had all at once been transformed into a hateful crone. I suggested that the least she could do was to put bells on the necks of her goats so that she would know where they were.

'Ah, no, zur, that woulden du, du 'ee zee?' she responded with a sweet effrontery the goats would have approved. 'Like that I'd have to du ·some'at about it if I was always to know where they were tu.'

'Depart from me, ye cursed, into everlasting fire, prepared for the devil and his angels!' I snarled at the beastly animals on the way home, whereupon they exchanged glances with each other and stared at me almost pityingly.

The only beneficiary will be my local ironmonger when I place an order for iron stakes and wire-mesh with which to barricade the banks.

✳

May is the month when one may have the good fortune to see fox-cubs on their first really serious venture into the hostile world around them; quite different from those peepings and scufflings that take place outside the earth when the cubs are still chubby, woolly, wide-eyed, sooty coloured bundles.

For anyone who is not simply content to watch from an arm-chair all the astonishing, immaculate, zoom-lens, celluloid products with which we are constantly regaled, animal-watching on one's own is a perfectly feasible matter. It needs common sense, enthusiasm, local knowledge, ability to read the wind and all the many signs of nature, and above all endless patience and a

(ABOVE) Free grazing for a herd of goats on Dartford Heath, Kent. Many specialists in the field of natural resources condemn the goat as Man's worst enemy. Indeed it was largely as a result of caprine depredations that much of the land bordering the Mediterranean was denuded of trees.

(*LEFT*) Man's first interest in the horse was as food. He hunted it long before he domesticated it. It is very likely that some of these moorland ponies will be exported and end up as horsemeat in France or Belgium.

Shakespeare's contemporary, Thomas Nash, had this to say about spring:

Spring, the sweet spring, is the
*   year's pleasant king;*
Then blooms each thing, then
*   maids dance in a ring,*
Cold doth not sting, the pretty
*   maids do sing:*
Cuckoo, jug, jug, pu we, to witta
*   woo!*

readiness to suffer certain discomforts in the shape of midges, pins-and-needles, cold, for example. A surprising amount of animal-watching can be done in daylight, especially in the long days of May and June.

It used to be thought by some naturalists that the dog-fox took no part in the rearing of the cubs. This is not so; the dog-fox is a devoted mate. In his *British Mammals*, Harrison Matthews even asserts that 'the male is monogamous and usually mates only once with his vixen; should his mate be killed he usually refuses to take another, forming an example of male faithfulness unknown in other wild animals.'

Be that as it may, as far as the cubs are concerned, the dog-fox not only plays an important part in providing for them, bringing food to the earth and dumping it for the vixen to collect, but he also helps with their education. Not long ago I had a vivid illustration of this.

After sunset I watched a vixen emerge from a spinney at the edge of a moorland field where I was hiding in the branches of a

fallen beech tree. She circled round a little distance, then loped back to the trees; it seemed that she had been disturbed. But she had been merely reconnoitring, for in a few moments she reappeared in company with five foxes, in such a formation that it was apparent a lesson of some sort was to take place.

Abreast and about forty yards apart were the vixen and a dog-fox; behind each of them, at intervals of a dozen yards or so, two cubs followed, imitating faithfully the movements of their parents. I watched the vixen, which was closer. Low-bellied, her legs obscured by the grass, she would run a few yards and halt, crouching behind an anthill or thistle-clump. Obviously not yet so skilful, the cubs followed suit, though sometimes one would continue to steal on a little farther, appropriately enough as if it were playing Sly Fox.

The vixen had all the appearance of stalking something specific. I waited for the deadly rush that would clinch the matter; but she went on in the same furtive manner. Near an ancient bury in the middle of the field a solitary rabbit still

Fox-cubs at play. W. H. Hudson once described a litter of cubs playing with a swede which they rolled here and there outside their earth until it went tumbling out of their reach down the sloping ground. By some means or another it had always been replaced by the next day for the cubs to resume their game.

lolloped about, not twenty yards from the vixen. Neither fox nor rabbit took any notice of each other: the vixen seemed to be concerned only with showing the cubs how to cover open ground as secretly as possible. There was something immensely thrilling at the sight of these six foxes making their stealthy, rapid progress. I was looking in on a private world.

While the dog-fox went farther downfield, the vixen skirted the bury and came in my direction. Thirty yards away she grew suspicious but not alarmed; a forepaw raised, she hesitated, questing the air. Obediently the cubs waited until their mother discreetly loped away. Guessing where they were heading, I left my hiding-place and, under cover of the tangled hedge and the rippling stream, I made a circuit of perhaps seventy yards. I had guessed right. There they were, nearer than ever; the whole family hunting separately: all six were engaged in pursuit of field-voles. Needless to say I could not see these, but it was quite clear what the foxes were after. Crouching, they would run with short rapid steps, pause, alert, then make a sudden pounce – they seem to use their forepaws in a stamping action rather than their teeth to pin down their prey. Hither and thither they made their crouching, eager, spasmodic way through the rough grass.

Sometimes the foxes would rear up, almost prance, on their hind legs, and scan the grass ahead of them, then, dropping down, hurry forward to pounce, guided perhaps by movements in the grass. Once the dog-fox became very excited over something. He leapt about, scraped the soil with his forepaws, reared up again, snuffled in the grass. A cub hastened to find what it was all about, but apparently was disappointed, for after he and his sire had consulted together he trotted off again to resume his own hunting.

Presently the family began to drift away, but one cub loped off in the direction of a rush-bed. I doubled back and reached a gate looking on to the rushes just as he showed up briefly on the left, walking leisurely along by the bank of the stream. While I squatted tight up against the stone gatepost he reappeared, casually inspecting anything he came across such as dried cow-pats. Quite unconcerned, he came by the gate. As he reached the post he caught sight of my boots. He halted, so close that I could have put my hand through the bars and touched him.

He stared and stared, trying to make things out. Then he flounced away a couple of yards and resumed his staring. There was no fear in his eyes; only puzzlement and curiosity. Few creatures are more beautiful than a fox-cub: slim and supple and altogether lovely. His throat and chest were white, but the rest of his coat was almost brindled, a sandy-brown interspersed with black and, round his shoulders, with darker brown, giving him a ragged, moulting appearance. Not for several weeks would his fur change to the familiar red.

Once more he flinched away; again he halted, triangular ears cocked, dark eyes staring. Then, deciding that my boots were too large to be trusted, he made off into the rushes, springily, lithely, head high in uneasiness, his whole manner strangely reminiscent of a deer, and so graceful and free as to cause me a pang at the thought of August with its misty mornings and the crash of hound-noise shattering the air.

✳

A feminine scream from upstairs – Murder? At the very least, surely, a burglar! Thunder of feet on the staircase, pounding to the rescue. Anti-climax. It's only a bat, a long-eared bat, in the bedroom. Useless to explain that it has probably followed a moth or beetle through the open window and if we don't fluster it by putting on the light or, crude thought, try to catch it with the landing-net, it will quickly find its way out again – without getting tangled in anyone's hair or committing other nuisances, not to speak of phlebotomizing us in our sleep.

The bat has intrigued men for centuries. Most puzzling of all was the true identity of this creature which flew as expertly as – indeed, more expertly than – a bird, and yet had the face and body of a very different beast. It was only in the sixteenth century that the Frenchman Pierre Belon, by dissecting a specimen, refuted the notion that the bat was a bird and showed that it was in fact a mammal.

Nevertheless, its sinister reputation persisted. Many superstitions surrounded it. It was suspect not only for its nightmare appearance but also for its uncanny haunts such as church-towers, dark caves and hollow trees; even for its abnormal manner of roosting upside down, shrouded in its wings. Like sundry other characters it was deemed fit only for a witch's brew.

> *Fillet of a fenny snake,*
> *In the caldron boil and bake;*
> *Eye of newt, and toe of frog,*
> *Wool of bat, and tongue of dog,*
> *Adder's fork and blindworm's sting,*
> *Lizard's leg, and howlet's wing –*

A 'hell-broth' indeed – a marvellous concoction!

But equally puzzling was how the bat could fly so accurately. 'As blind as a bat' is a familiar saying, though without foundation. The bat does possess eyes, but these are of little use, simply allowing it to distinguish between dark and light. How does it fly with such pin-point skill? William Collins gives us a clue:

> *Now air is hushed, save where the weak-eyed bat,*
> *With short shrill shriek flies by on leathern wing.*

Nearly two hundred years ago, the Italian naturalist, Lazaro Spallanzani, by means of some rather gruesome experiments,

The greater horseshoe bat (*Rhinolophus ferrum-equinum*) is named for its horseshoe-shaped nose-leaf. It has a wing-span of thirteen inches and flies at a very low level, just two or three feet above the ground. It is, however, a very strong flier; in one experiment a horseshoe bat was found to have made a flight of forty miles.

proved that bats do not rely on sight for navigating. He blinded a number of them and found that they could perfectly well manoeuvre in flight even though they were truly sightless. Not until the present century, however, was it established that the bat possesses a kind of ultrasonic equipment. It is able to send out short wave-length squeaks or pulses, the reflected echoes from which provide information about the nature and position of surrounding objects. These squeaks, too high-pitched for the human ear, are sent out at the rate of about thirty per second, and the faster the squeak-rate the more information comes back to the flying bat. It is this which enables the bat not only to avoid colliding with other bats or blundering into wall or post – or nervous human being – but to hunt moths, beetles, flies, so deftly.

That long-eared bat, which caused such a domestic brouha-ha, roosts in the loft of my house, as do various pipistrelles, smallest of all the bats. Sometimes at dusk I watch them come sliding out of the eaves as unobtrusively as leaves fluttering on the air. In these fragrant May evenings there is no lack of prey for them. To most people a bat is a bat is a bat; in fact there are twelve British species. They range from the serotine, which has a heavy, mothlike flight, to the noctule or great bat which is as agile as the swifts with which it hunts far up in the sky.

But the bat I enjoy watching most, when I can, is Daubenton's. It likes to hunt over water, circling very low above the surface. Once, on the River Test in Hampshire, I was startled, delighted, to see suddenly literally scores of Daubenton's bats appear as if at the raising of the curtain on some fairy scene. The air was full of them and one was almost bewildered by these silent, fluttering, supremely expert wings all around. With that evocative, ineffable scent of water, the scent of honeysuckle, the sound of unseen cows munching contentedly nearby in the twilight, a church-tower silhouetted against the glowing sky, a late-fishing heron flapping away, gigantic in comparison with those tiny bats, a corncrake rasping, swifts screaming overhead like anxious prompters, it was straight out of the world of Puck and Titania – and I swear I heard a music that never Mendelssohn wrote!

For a long time the flock of bats flickered, swooped, doubled, dived, sometimes actually breaking the surface of the river to catch water-insects – and every now and then there would be the plop of a trout, perhaps jumping up to see what on earth was going on. Then, all of a sudden, just as abruptly as they had appeared, those little bats vanished. Their aerial ballet was over, the play was done. They had gone off to another beat. And in that summer sky the first star hung large and gently molten, as if to light the audience home.

*

The gamekeeper's gibbet: on the extreme left is a rat, then some squirrels; hanging on the extreme right are magpies and jays. Man classifies as vermin anything 'inimical' to his paramount interests.

*And many other beasts
And birds, skin, bone and feather,
Have been taken from their feasts
And hung up there together.*

All the better-known bird-singers have had their admirers and have been immortalized in poetry – and often in music. Keats's *Ode to a Nightingale* is the classic example, though many would consider the nightingale's song little if at all, superior, to the blackcap's rippling tunes or the blackbird's mellow, leisured fluting. But night adds romance to its 'melodious sorrows' and there is then more likelihood of 'magic casements opening on the foam', for its song makes less impression in daytime – though nothing can cause such a pang as that long-drawn, plaintive, throbbing (almost sobbing) *pew pew pew* that climbs to a heart-stirring crescendo. Clare said of the nightingale:

*When first we heard the shy-come nightingales,
They seem to mutter o'er their songs in fear,*

And, climb we e'er so soft the spinney rails,
All stops as if no bird was anywhere.

Yet, by contrast, the nightingale can sometimes be startled into song by a sudden noise just as, to go off at a slight tangent, thunder will set cock-pheasants crowing.

The skylark's 'silver chain of sound, Of many links without a break' inspired not only Shelley but Vaughan Williams in his exquisite *Lark Ascending,* that lovely evocation. And tributes to the cuckoo were not confined to Wordsworth's 'blithe new-comer' of the 'wandering voice', for the bird also inspired Delius to compose his gentle tribute to the English summer. Incidentally, the cuckoo *does* sing. In days when this intriguing parasite was far more numerous, I have heard cuckoos singing against one another – and I cannot express it better than did E. W. Hendy in his *Bird Watching* half a century ago:

> *One day my wife and I listened to three cuckoos singing*
> *together: one sang a major, one a minor third, and*
> *another a perfect fourth. Two of these were calling at a*
> *different pitch, the one much higher than the other, so*
> *that the 'coo' of the tenor cuckoo was the same note as*
> *the 'cuck' of the bass!*

The songs of chaffinch, linnet, blackbird, song-thrush, robin – tributes have been paid to them all by Shakespeare, Blake, Browning, Meredith, Yeats. Yet there are two minor songs which are passed by, of which I am particularly fond. This morning a pair of swallows, which have been prospecting the shippon, settled in an appletree almost overhead and sat facing each other as if by pre-arrangement, while the male bird sang his twittering, low-pitched song. The range of it was only a few notes, but it was infinitely sweet and intimate, like drops of dew. *Seeta feeta feetit, seeta feeta feetit* is the nearest I can get to it. Attentively the female swallow listened and when he had finished his tiny protestation the pair flung themselves ecstatically into the air and curved away among the trees in an even more wonderful 'song', if in a different form.

Then in the evening down in the valley after dusk, I heard the 'brown evejar', the nightjar, uttering its incomparable purring, softly trilling murmur that is so redolent of a night in May which even in these tired days can still contain magic, dreamlike moments.

June

Mr Maddowcroft has shorn his sheep. The last night or two have been loud with the bleating of the penned-up animals, hungry and thirsty, pestered by flies, with ewe separated from lamb in the churning mob. Now they are shorn they are bleating almost as plaintively, partly, no doubt, because the weather having turned fresher they feel the lack of their thick fleeces – though during the hot days immediately before the shearing they spent much of the time panting in the shade of the oak-trees. But some of the bleating is caused by uncertainty over scent-recognition now their fleeces have been stripped from them. Sheep are always at their most restless after being shorn, so watch out for your garden banks and fences. The yocs, as Mr Maddowcroft calls them, look strangely naked, and are as creamy-white as the late-flowering hawthorns that dot the hillside.

No outside gang-work for Mr Maddowcroft; he and his family and one or two cronies do it all themselves, down to Jane who staggers out with a wicker-clad jar of scrumpy and Missus who toils over the Rayburn to feed us all (spectators included) at the end of the day. Shearing always used to be the occasion for a feast, accompanied by sheep-shearing songs and pastoral revelry under the command of the elected king and queen of the shearers. In spite of all the toil and sweat, work like this was a festival, something to be enjoyed in company with your friends and neighbours, as it still is in peasant countries.

Now each yoe is manhandled to the shearer in the barn, deftly thrown on its back and, with the electric clippers burring away, Mr Maddowcroft or Frank his son-in-law starts at the throat, clears the neck and shoulders with an aplomb that makes the layman wince, expecting veins or arteries to be gashed open at any moment. Rarely is there even a nick and that is quickly dealt with by a dab of tar, an old remedy still in use.

Now the shearer is cutting along the belly and over the ribs, down the thighs, over the rump. Over he turns the strangely quiescent ewe ('as a sheep before her shearers is dumb') and the clippers are shearing through the wool of the back. It's done almost before a man can refill his pipe. Well, not quite, but well under ten minutes. Faster than Gabriel Oak who took 'three-and-twenty minutes and a half', but then of course he was only using hand-shears. As Hardy wrote:

The clean, sleek creature arose from its fleece – how perfectly like Aphrodite rising from the foam should have

and body, with her depressed bill sometimes helping to keep it in position during the flight.

✳

For me, when I was young, one of the most spectacular, beautiful and deliciously terrifying summertime creatures was, indeed, still is, the dragonfly. Partly it was its name, as evocative as 'foxglove'; mainly it was its appearance. Few natural phenomena, at least to a child, could be more imposing, menacing even, than that huge insect with its equally enormous gig-lamp eyes, its shimmering colours, sometimes emerald-green or metallic blue or waspish yellow and brown, and its gauzy, delicately netted wings, its slow, deliberate, spasmodic flight interspersed with sudden awful zipping sallies at top speed.

Moreover, when you discovered that the dragonfly could actually fly backwards, you were even more impressed. You watched in fascination tinged with caution as it manoeuvred over the purple loosestrife and the yellow flags and the sculpted water. We were quite convinced that it could sting, a fallacy reinforced by the two suspicious-looking appendages on its tail. We used to call dragonflies 'horsestingers' and there was a verse based on this belief. In later years I was delighted to come across another version of it in Walter de la Mare's *Come Hither:*

> *Snakestanger, snakestanger, vlee aal about the brooks;*
> *Sting aal the bad bwoys that vor the fish looks,*
> *But let the good bwoys ketch aal the vish they can,*
> *And car'm away whooam to vry 'em in a pan;*
> *Bread and butter they shall yeat at supper wi' their vish*
> *While aal the littul bad bwoys shall only lick the dish.*

However, stingless though the dragonfly is, it is a voracious hunter, and its chief object in life is to satisfy its insatiable appetite. Among its favourite prey are horseflies – grey flies or clegs, those real stingers that can stampede cattle or make some people swell up painfully. The dragonfly catches its prey by means of its forward-acting, hairy legs which form an efficient net or grab, then it zooms down to a suitable landing-place, and tears off the insect's wings in its jaws before starting on the meal. Some of the larger dragonflies will kill wasps and butterflies of tortoiseshell size.

But pirate of the air that the adult is, almost more formidable in its own small world is its larva. The female dragonfly lays her eggs sometimes simply by dropping them in water, sometimes by inserting them individually in the stems of aquatic plants – after which the attendant male helps to drag her out of the water. The infant dragonfly is, bizarrely, called a nymph, but nothing could be less like the conventional 'nymph more bright than moonshine night'.

It is the terror of the waters it frequents and the larger ones even catch tadpoles and fish-fry. Mostly it waits in ambush or crawls about in search of prey; but it can move fast at times by means of jet propulsion, squirting water from its vent. It is armed with a so-called 'mask', an extension of its lower jaws which shoot out to snatch its victim with disproportionately large and deadly pincers. Afterwards the mask is folded away neatly under the head.

In some of the larger species the nymph remains in this underwater form for two or three years, repeatedly changing its skin as it grows. When the time for metamorphosis arrives, it ceases to breathe through its gills and instead takes in air through spiracles or breathing-holes. It now crawls out on to the stem of a plant and the chitinous skin begins to crack, enabling the newly-created dragonfly to emerge. The characteristic long tail comes out last and grows rapidly, sometimes to a size far greater than the abandoned nymphal case. The wings expand and harden and within two or three hours the nymph is transformed into a dragon of the brookside. As in Francis Brett Young's *Bête Humaine:*

Lo, the bright air alive with dragonflies;
With brittle wings aquiver, and great eyes
Piloting crimson bodies, slender and gay.

But what of those prehistoric dragonflies, with a wingspan of two feet, the largest insect that ever existed? With what scintillating colours must *they* have painted the air millions of years ago!

✢

One of my earliest memories is of an old countrywoman sedulously banging a tin tray with a coal-shovel to stop a swarm of bees from moving away from where they had settled before their owner, her son, could come and retrieve them. It was also believed that if this ritual was not carried out no legal claim could be made to the bees should they end up on someone else's property. Later, when one of my brothers took to keeping bees, I had to play a hose on a swarm until he could arrive to hive them.

For it was at this season that a swarm was considered most valuable, and still is.

A swarm of bees in May
Is worth a load of hay.
A swarm of bees in June
Is worth a silver spoon.
A swarm of bees in July
Is scarcely worth a fly.

June is certainly the most auspicious month for bees to swarm, if they are going to at all; it is now that they have the best chance of

A dragonfly only develops the full beauty of its colouring several hours after its metamorphosis. This photograph reveals clearly the gauzy translucence of the insect's wings.

A swarm of honeybees *(Apis mellifera)* hanging from the branch of a tree. According to old beekeepers, one reason bees are less likely to sting during swarming is that their abdomens are so distended with honey that stinging becomes impossible.

establishing or re-establishing themselves. During the early summer months in a good year the numbers in a hive may rise to as many as eighty thousand and it rapidly becomes overcrowded. Swarming is simply an intelligent, if instinctive, action on the part of some of the bees to avert disaster, which would inevitably follow if such numbers remained unchecked. Emigration is the human equivalent, but we are not so well organized as the bees.

It is always the old queen who leads the swarm and before the hour of departure she and the many thousands of bees that are going to accompany her gorge themselves on honey to sustain them until they settle in a new home. There is a frenzied bustle of excitement, an unmistakable menacing hum, and the air is scribbled with the to-ings and fro-ings of the insects as the swarm prepares to move off in a compact mass. Yet strangely enough, at the time of the swarm the bees are at their most docile – a fact proved by photographs of bee-keepers draped or bearded with a swarm, from which they suffer not a single sting.

The remainder of the colony become the subjects of a new monarch; a young queen having been elevated to the throne by being fed as a grub with 'royal jelly'. Some women pay vast sums

for this fluid, produced in the heads of bees, in the hope that it will help them retain their good looks and prolong their life.

Not a single one of the queen-bee's thirty thousand subjects is entirely idle. Even the several hundred drones, whose name is wrongly linked with uselessness, fulfil the vital function of mating with the queen. As for the worker-bees, their six-week working life is crammed with activity. After the honey-scouts have come back and performed their complicated dance by which they impart news of nectar, its direction and distance, the main body of workers wing ceaselessly to and fro with their loads, beating their wings more than eleven thousand times a minute. Inside the hive, other bees are constantly at work constructiong the marvellous and intricate honeycomb which is a masterpiece of engineering and will support twenty-five times its own weight. Other bees act as nursemaids to the grubs or stand on guard at the entrance. Yet others act as scavengers; if any intruders such as snails or mice die inside a badly kept hive and are too heavy to move, these scavenger bees mummify the bodies with a special hygienic glue.

It is this orderly, intense communal life that so fascinates the

Beekeepers in Ancient Greece used to shave their heads before working at the hives. They believed that the perfume of their hair irritated the bees, making them more likely to sting. Modern apiarists find a hat and veil a more practical solution.

bee-keeper and evokes his admiration. There is indeed something wonderful and magic in the way this insignificant insect, half an inch long, can suck nectar from the loveliest flowers and turn it, through the alchemy of its body, into a nourishing and perfectly balanced food.

*

Anyone with a hedgehog in his garden can count himself lucky. Together with birds such as the song-thrush it does an immense amount of good taking slugs, snails and insects. The one drawback is that the hedgehog will also kill frogs and toads, those other friends of the gardener. Needless to say, it doesn't happen in the garden, but the hedgehog will also tackle snakes – not only the grass-snake but the viper as well. It is said to be immune to the viper's poison, but in any case, when attacked by the hedgehog the snake lacerates itself in vain against its adversary's spines.

Many people have a hedgehog-tenant without being aware of it – unless they put out a nightly saucer of bread and milk and know that it isn't the cat which has gratefully emptied it by the next morning. Occasionally you get a glimpse of the visitors and one night this month I watched a mother and four young hedgehogs contentedly supping together near the back doorstep. Another night I heard the young ones twittering anxiously like strange birds. I hope nothing has happened to their mother.

At birth the hedgehog's spines are soft and white, but after a month or so they change colour and harden into the familiar protective coat which is unlike that of any other animal. The hedgehog can erect its spines at will and can of course roll itself into a tight, compact ball at the onset of danger. This is proof against many enemies such as dogs, whose frustrated barking in a field at night is often the result of their finding a hedgehog and not knowing how to deal with it, but not, alas, against motor-cars, while fox and badger have little difficulty circumventing that spiny armour – the badger simply biting right through it. As for gypsies, traditionally they have had a passion for hedgehog meat; they plaster an animal with clay, roast it over the camp-fire, and when it is done, the clay and the spines peel away together.

The urchin or hedgepig, two of the hedgehog's aliases, used to be accused of sucking the milk from cows. To refute that it is only necessary to compare the size of the animal's mouth with a cow's teat. The truth of the matter is probably that milk sometimes dribbles from the overful udder of a cow, and the hedgehog, through its keen sense of smell, is drawn towards it. In addition, it may well frequent grazing cows in search of the beetles and other insects likely to be working on the cow-pats.

Ever since the days of Pliny, the hedgehog has been credited with the knack of carrying away apples, pears and strawberries

If the pear on which this hedgehog is feasting is over-ripe he may well end up drunk. As for the tarrydiddle that hedgehogs milk cows, John Clare comments:

*But they who've seen the small
   head like a hog
Rolled up to meet the savage of a
   dog
With mouth scarce big enough to
   hold a straw
Will ne'er believe what no one ever
   saw.*

on its spines. In the case of apples it was said to climb trees to fetch the fruit, or to fling itself on its back and impale windfalls. It is a yarn that keeps cropping up, but has never been authenticated. And nobody has explained how the hedgehog unloads the fruit afterwards. In any case, the hedgehog's diet is almost entirely carnivorous – even carrion is not despised.

✳

The slow-worm lay still, as if death had touched it as it made its humble way across the track, taking refuge in immobility at the sound or vibration of my footsteps. Its slender body was like a casting in bronze: its back a coppery shade, its well defined sides almost brick-red, its skin shining with a glaze like that on pottery. Tiny black eyes alone revealed the fact that it was a living creature. Was it too much to feel that I could see apprehension in them, as if the slow-worm sensed only too well the fate usually meted out to its kind?

For minutes on end the illusion of lifelessness persisted. It was as if the slim, elaborate handle of a vase fashioned out of some rare, highly polished stone had been discarded. Yes, it was more like that than the casting in bronze which had first occurred to me. And apart from the strange beauty of that lowly body, the way in which it retained for so long its absolute immobility was a cause for wonder. With what subtle and vastly different methods of defence Nature endows her creatures.

But what unloving, unseeing eye dubbed this particular creature 'slow-worm', when it is no worm, certainly is not always

The honeysuckle *(Lonicera periclymemum)* is a flower that appears to have come straight out of the fairy world of Puck and Titania and is redolent of the English summer.

slow, and can glide with snakelike grace? Or blind-worm, with its small, bright eyes so evident? Few people are familiar with the slow-worm. It is secretive in its ways, though like so many animals, including Man, it enjoys basking in the sun, and when one is discovered the common human urge is to stamp on it.

This attitude could not have been better illustrated as I contemplated the slow-worm in the cart-track. A boy of thirteen or fourteen trudged up the hill, accompanied by two smaller children. They halted, curious to know what I was doing, crouching on the ground. Catching sight of the slow-worm, they began to nudge each other and whisper, amidst a great deal of heavy breathing.

'That's a snake!' the boy warned me, sternly, as if to say I was aiding and abetting a criminal.

'I don't vancy 'e!' muttered one of the others, backing away. I was not certain whether he was referring to me or the slow-worm.

I tried to explain that the slow-worm was neither worm nor snake, but in fact a lizard, which had lost its legs in the course of

The downy rose (*Rosa tomentosa*) is so called because both sides of its leaves have a downy texture.

evolution. I would have liked to explain that it had eyelids as other lizards do, that its small black tongue was notched, not forked, that the sides of its lower jaw were united in front, all attributes alien to the snake; in face of a battery of disapproving eyes, I faltered. In any case, the sturdy voice of realism broke in.

'Be going to kill 'un?' demanded the boy and, on my declining, he volunteered to do it himself. 'Our dad put spade through a couple last Sunday.'

I took the quiescent slow-worm in my hands, though this symbolic gesture was quite involuntary and inspired much uneasy mumbling and shuffling. Plainly my audience regarded me as more sinister than the 'snake' itself, and forthwith stumped off up the hill. A backward glance and a furtive guffaw summed it all up. I felt depressed at my feeble powers of persuasion.

But for the fact that the slow-worm manifested surprising strength and litheness in trying to slip through my fingers, the illusion of polished stone would have remained. Its scales were so close-set, lacking the rough 'keels' of the grass-snake, and so exquisitely smooth, that its skin seemed one continuous piece.

Although the slow-worm is a lizard its scientific name is *Anguis fragilis* – the fragile snake. It was so-named because it has the ability to cast off its tail in an emergency. After the old tail has been cast a new one is grown although it never attains the same length as the original.

One attribute it has in common with snakes – it casts its skin three or four times a year, according to the plenitude or dearth of slugs, its principal food. The sloughing is in response to the need for more room for its growing body.

When I put it down again it lay still for a while, twelve inches of sinuous immobility. Then, tentatively, black tongue flickering at intervals, it made its way across the track and, approaching the fern-hung bank, glided out of sight with sudden graceful speed.

July

This could be called a ghost-story — and I see the ghosts whenever I give Mr Maddowcroft a hand with his haymaking: he's late this year, but then, as Vita Sackville-West says in *The Land*

> *'Tis farmer, not the date, that calls the tune;*
> *Better dry August hay than wet in June.*

But at least it is not yet August, it is still only the beginning of July.

Towed by the blue tractor, the red binding-machine goes rattling and yawing and thumping rhythmically round the cut meadow, eating up the silky swaths that look so much thicker than when the grass was standing, pricked out by trefoil and chickweed. Like some monster with an insatiable appetite, it takes them up, processes them through its mechanical belly and ejects them in a totally different form — gigantic slab-shaped pellets from an iron predator. Neat and precise but green and unripe-looking, the bales bump along the tail-ramp and topple out regularly one after the other, as if from a conveyor-belt.

The blue fumes of the tractor stifle the fragrance of the hay and drive away the puzzled bumble-bees. The wild roses in the hedgeside droop as if overcome. As the shadows lengthen, the field is dotted with hundreds of oblong packages which, as we prop them up to air one against the other, look like weird, drunken figures out of some cubist fantasy.

But in my mind's eye I see quite other figures — nutbrown men in braces — heaving stagger-sized fork-loads of hay which are impressive not only for their size but for the way in which they stay on the two-pronged forks while they are levered up, brandished almost like huge, proud, rustic gonfalons, to the man who is loading. Half my fork-loads used to come tumbling ignominiously about my ears, making me sneeze so that by the time I had recovered the waggon had moved on thirty yards.

There are other figures, too — women in wide-brimmed straw-hats — raking together the remains of the swaths so that not a wisp is left. But the ghosts I chiefly see are riding on top of the last drunkenly swaying load piled perilously high on the waggon. They are children, hanging on for life and limb, almost buried in the hay, only their heads visible, like elfin spirits of the haysel, squealing in mingled triumph, delight and apprehension

Stacking the hay: a scene that might have come straight out of *Lark Rise to Candleford*. Flora Thompson would not have been surprised at the number of men working here, though nowadays people aren't used to such a sight.

as the horses clump steadily on through the narrow lanes, leaving a tribute of hay on the hedgrows as they pass.

It is a scene that Edward Thomas saw —

Older than Clare and Cobbett, Morland and Crome,
Than, at the field's far edge, the farmer's home,
A white house crouched at the foot of a great tree.

You could still see it up to the post-war years when machines finally took over on the farm. It is not the same, riding on a load of bales behind a stinking tractor.

*

In the valley these warm evenings among the heather there appear almost as regularly as if switched on, tiny, exquisite, lambent green beacons. They are the signals emitted by glow-worms, which are not 'worms', but a kind of beetle in spite of their name. Only the female of the species can produce light; she is an uncomely, drab, grey, grublike creature not even able to fly — though she shares that disability with some other beetles. But she is redeemed by that magic, radiant, dreamlike light which is redolent of the world of Puck. Though it is not, as Titania thought, 'the fiery glow-worm's eyes' that cause the light; it

comes from the last three segments of the insect's body. Less alluring than her light is the glow-worm's use of an anaesthetic with which she first paralyses then transforms into a jellylike substance the snails she feeds on.

*

When I call my pigs, they will come charging joyfully towards me from three or four hundred yards away, though it has to be admitted that my stentorian cries of 'Chug chug chug!' are often reinforced by the clanging of a bucket; pigs will follow a bucket anywhere, especially if there is a bait of potatoes in it. Once upon a time I used to lead the individual sows to a stud-boar nearly a mile away like that, including crossing the A30 – though I wouldn't dare do it nowadays.

As I summon them now, I am reminded of *Life Begins at Forty* a splendid film of a good many years ago. Set in the American mid-west, one of its central features was a hog-calling contest in which pigs were conjured up from prodigious distances by those peerless comedians Will Rogers and Slim Summerville.

In modern farming, gathering in animals by special calls has largely gone by the board, along with hand-milking and butter-tubs. What, for instance, do they call calves in veal-factories as they crowd in knock-kneed and lightless misery? Do they say 'Chook chook chooky' in broiler houses? The birds wouldn't understand – factory hens have even lost the savoir-faire to scratch!

There used to be a great variety of calls for the pig, varying according to the part of the country. 'Giss! Giss! Gissy!' I have heard that uttered in recent times; 'Lix!', 'Ric-sic!' 'Dack dack

(ABOVE) A female glow-worm *(Lampyris noctiluca)*. Walter de la Mare once described how he had enjoyed the curious pleasure of reading a little book in small print by glow-worm light. 'The glow-worm was lifting its green beam in the grasses of a cliff by the sea, and shone the clearer the while because it was during an eclipse of the moon.'

(ABOVE, LEFT) Well, all the beautiful people believe in mud-packs.

(LEFT) Haycocks are rare nowadays but they can still be seen in Scotland. These were photographed on a croft in Glencoe.

(ABOVE) Hay being harvested on Exmoor.

When hay was stored in ricks it had to be much riper and drier than is necessary now that it is baled for there was always a danger of rick fires breaking out as a result of spontaneous combustion within the rick.

dack!' But best of all to my mind is 'Tantassa, tantassa pig, tow-a-row, a-row! Tig, tig, tig!' I can just see the pigs pricking up their ears, grunting excitedly, kicking their heels, and converging pell-mell on the caller. All with curly tails, of course, as befits a healthy pig.

In Elizabeth Mary Wright's classic *Rustic Speech and Folklore*, there is a splendid catalogue of farm-calls. Turkeys were addressed thus: 'Cobbler! Peet peet peet! Pen! Pur pur pur!'; after them waddled the geese, their usual stately progress made more urgent by cries of 'Fy-laig! Gag gag gag! Ob-ee! White-hoddy! White-hoddy!'; and the softly quacking ducks responded to 'Bid bid bid! Diddle! Dill, dill! Wid, Wheetie!' As for sheep, their call-sign was 'Ovey ovey ovey!' which is surely an echo of the Latin for sheep – *ovis*. But imbued with earthy wisdom though he is, one would not expect the shepherd to be acquainted with such nomenclature.

Even pigeons and rabbits had their calls, but this was really a matter of friendly conversation rather than actually calling them up. You said to the pigeon in its loft, 'Pees! Pod! Pees! Pod!' while 'Map map map!' was your greeting to the rabbit humpling to the door of its hutch to receive a bundle of dandelions and clover.

But for me the quintessential farmyard cry was in calling up the cows at milking-time. 'Coop coop coop!' I would cry, standing importantly by the open gate. 'Cush cush cush!' I was fourteen at the time and in love with a milkmaid and it used to

This photograph provides a nice contrast to the one on the opposite page and together they show how radically farming has changed during the twentieth century. Here a farm worker returns after the evening's milking.

make my day to hear her calling 'Mull! Mull! Mully!' and 'Proo! Proochy! Prut!' splendidly rolling those tight 'r's. I never minded that Gretchen, Bluebell, Brownie and all the rest who had stared in dewy-eyed disdain at my crack-voiced summons should now come ambling full-uddered through the buttercups, their breath laden with the fragrance of summer grass.

That milkmaid had special old-fashioned calls for calves, too. 'Mog mog mog!' was one of them and only her voice could make attractive such an unpromising monosyllable. When she was feeding them, trying to make them drink out of a bucket with her fingers for encouragement, she would say appropriately, 'Sook, sook, sook!'

But then, in days when hedgerows were permanently festooned with foxgloves and wild roses and honeysuckle, the milkmaid was a symbol of natural charm. As the Elizabethan Sir Thomas Overbury put it: 'A Fair and Happy Milk-maid is a Country Wench that is so far from making herself beautiful by art, that one look at hers is able to put all face-physic out of countenance'.

Horses cannot be omitted from a catalogue of farm-calls, though of course in their case it was mainly a question of directions or commands. Their origins lost in the mists of time, the most familiar are 'Gee-up!' accompanied by the clicking of the tongue, while 'Whoa!' brought the horse to a standstill.

Some, such as 'Hait!', 'Keep!' and 'Joss!' were used in Chaucer's time. The significance of others, such as 'Mock-mether-hauve!' or 'Wo-cum-huggin!' was no doubt obvious to the horse, but would need interpretation by ploughman, carter or stablehand for the benefit of the layman.

*

Yesterday a brood of ducklings hatched out. Eight of them, deep primrose-yellow, arranged in a cosy ring of delightful, almost contrived, charm – ducklings in any case are far more attractive than baby chicks.

By this morning all but two had disappeared, taken by rats – it couldn't have been anything else. The mother-duck was not hysterical, as a hen would have been – just bewildered, speaking in an undertone and cocking a black eye as if to make sure she was not going to get the blame.

I like to credit myself with being quite objective towards all wildlife, but have to admit to a certain uneasiness about rats. They are formidable creatures and not merely because of their numbers. 'Cunning rat' is more accurate than the rat as a symbol of cowardice, e.g. 'rats leaving a sinking ship', after all, what sensible person wouldn't, if he had the chance. A cornered rat is not to be easily dismissed and I remember one that leapt at the

Seventy years ago, when the photograph on the opposite page was taken, a farmer *might* have got six hundred gallons of milk a year from each of his cows. The Friesians in this ultra-modern milking-unit may each produce well over two thousand gallons a year.

(LEFT) The foxglove *(Digitalis purpurea)* has many aliases: dead man's bells, finger-flower, flap dock, witches' bells.

(RIGHT) Ducks always seem to have a much greater sense of enjoyment than hens. They also have a habit of wandering far and near which often leads them into trouble.

throat of a friend of mine who suffered from a septic wound for some time afterwards. Although it is fair to say that the rat was probably not attacking its assailant, but trying to leap over her shoulder as she stooped to hit it. Occasionally, a rat will stand up to a ferret, and when ferrets were muzzled, many a rat made a successful, savage and fatal counter-attack.

The brown rat, which is the one I am concerned with here, only took up residence in Britain about 250 years ago. Being more fecund and aggressive it ousted the so-called 'native' black rat, whose chief claim to fame was as a carrier of the bubonic plague, the 'Black Death' which decimated the human population time after time. ('A dreadful plague in London was, In the year sixty-five, Which swept an hundred thousand souls Away; yet I alive!') The black rat itself, which is smaller and more slender than the brown, probably only reached this country round about the twelfth century; legend has it that it arrived in the ships of returning crusaders. Nowadays it still exists in small numbers in various sea-ports and no doubt is still shipborne.

The brown rat population seems to have irrupted in Central Asia in the late seventeenth and early eighteenth centuries. The naturalist Thomas Pennant estimated the species' arrival in Britain at about 1720, while fervent Jacobites, notably the peerless Charles Waterton, were convinced it accompanied George I and dubbed it the Hanoverian rat. ('It actually came over in the same ship that conveyed the new dynasty to these shores.') The less partisan called it the Norway rat.

There is something disturbing about rats; perhaps it is their furtive skulking ways, their association with dubious haunts such as sewers. In fact the rat is a scrupulously clean animal in the way it grooms itself; it has even been known to groom itself between attacks by a ferret. At times you can sense the presence of rats even though you do not actually see them; at other times their sheer numbers force their attention on you. Once I witnessed a 'rat-flit'. Not far from the Sussex farm where I once worked, there was a slaughterhouse. One night this caught fire. I was walking home at the time and stopped to watch the blaze. To get a better view I climbed on to a cart shed and was thankful to have done so. For presently I became aware of a strangely unnerving sound and looking down was aware of a great number of rats making their way past. I don't know how many there were of them, certainly scores, but it seemed hundreds and I could see their eyes glinting as they hurried on. I stayed a long time after the fire had subsided before venturing down.

Nothing is safe from the rat; it can swim expertly, climb with ease, swarm along telegraph wires, gnaw its way through concrete blocks or lead water-pipes. It is omnivorous: fish, fowl, flesh, vegetable, mollusc, all are equally acceptable; it will cheerfully turn cannibal, too. And it is ubiquitous: on various remote islands, wildlife has been seriously affected by it. But of course it lives most fatly in the presence of Man; it is currently estimated by the United Nations Environment Secretariat that rats consume enough of Man's annual farm-produce to feed 200 million people and that if adequate attention was paid to storing grain the world food outlook would be radically different.

Well, I suppose if I had adequately protected my golden-yellow ducklings...

*

Once long ago as I was walking along a lane, there rang out from the field close by a shrill, wailing scream. It could only have been made by a rabbit being assaulted by a stoat. I clambered over a gate and legged it towards the place the sound had come from.

Immobilized by terror, the rabbit was huddled by the hedge. The stoat, alarmed by my approach, had disappeared. But in a few moments, in the characteristic manner of his kind, he emerged, chakkering resentfully, and only retreated at a near miss from a stick. Before long the rabbit came to again and presently humpled away, safe at least for the time being, while I self-righteously resumed my walk.

I would not interfere like that nowadays. I might hurry towards the spot, but only in the hope of watching the stoat at work, not to save the rabbit. I was reminded of all this early one morning when I sat and watched a hedgehog consuming a frog. A callous attitude on my part? I think not. What right had I to interfere in a natural process? Wild animals hunt only to obtain food; there is no such thing as cruelty in nature. The stoat killing the rabbit, the hedgehog munching the living frog, spider sucking the life-juices of a moth, sparrowhawk striking down a song-bird, all are acting only in the way there were created to act, and death to one creature is life to another. It is a continuing circle, starting – and ending – with the worm. Or, as Emerson's Brahma saw it, it is all a case of

How lizard fed on ant, and snake on him,
And kite on both; and how the fish-hawk robbed
The fish-tiger of that which it had seized;
The shrike chasing the bulbul, which did hunt
The jewelled butterflies; till everywhere
Each slew a slayer and in turn was slain,
Life living upon death.

Only Man is consciously cruel; only Man hunts for sport or profit; only man has wiped out whole orders of bird and beast. No wild predator has ever caused the extinction of a single species.

✻

A mystery: a hen's egg neatly ensconced in a little hollow under the exposed roots of an old appletree. No hen was small enough to have laid there, for the roots grew in the form of a claw under which she could not have crept. Any thieving magpie or crow would have eaten the egg on the spot. In any case, the laying-box was inside the shippon, almost ten yards away. So who or what was responsible?

At once I called to mind stories of rats using hen-houses as a kind of take-away establishment. There is no disputing the fact that rats are capable of removing eggs intact; it is the method which has for long been the subject of argument. Some observers claim that they roll the egg away with their chin or tucked between chin and forepaws. But the favourite story is typified by an account that appeared in *The Zoologist* over a hundred years ago.

The rector of a parish in Westmorland assured me that he
had witnessed this feat. Having lost many eggs belonging
to a laying hen, he was induced to watch to discover the
thief. One morning, soon after the cackling bird had
given warning that she had deposited an egg, he observed
two rats come out of a hole in the hen-house and proceed
direct to the nest. One of the rats then lay down on its
side, while the other rat rolled the egg so near it that it
could embrace it with his feet. Having now obtained a
secure hold on its egg, its companion dragged it into the
hole by its tail, and disappeared.

This prototype tale has been repeated ad infinitum. Unfortunately no reputable and completely reliable naturalist has observed the feat, while the 'witnesses' who have claimed to see it all omit to record how the second rat pulled the transporter-rat along.

The word 'barn' is derived from the Old English *bere-ern*, 'the barley place'. But the Dutch barn (shown on the left in this photograph), which has been widely adopted in this country, is only useful for storing hay or straw. Nothing has ever really taken the place of the traditional barn, shown here on the right partly hidden by trees.

They talk of its standing erect and holding the tail over its shoulder, but presumably not even the Westmorland parson would have suggested that it held the tail in its paws. A recumbent rat would have been a hefty weight for another to haul and the latter's teeth would have exerted a painful grip on the transporter-rat's tail.

In *Animal Legends,* the late Maurice Burton provides a variation on the story. He received it in a letter from a correspondent in Gloucestershire and once again it is at second hand, indeed third hand.

> This account was given to me by a mason who was working for a local farmer doing repairs to a barn. The farmer asked him if he would like to see something unusual and took him up to the loft above his stable. 'He bade me be quiet and look down through a knot-hole in the floor, so I did and there was a hen in the manger, sitting wide up in the corner. In a few minutes, up she got clacking like they do and then perched on the manger and flew off. Farmer put up his hand to keep me quiet and in a couple of minutes I could see a rat coming up the post and then another one following him up into the manger. Then they got the egg out of the bit of nest-hay and each of the rats rolled it up on the ledge of the manger by their forepaws helped by their hindlegs. When the egg was

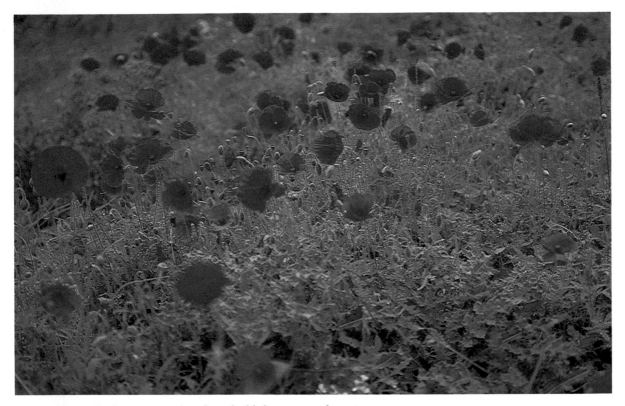

safely rolled up on to this flat shelf they waited a minute, and then one rat lay down on his back and the other rolled the egg on to the one who was lying down. He at once clasped it safely between fore and back paws, where it lay as in a square furry cup. As both rats were on the flat shelf it was quite easy for the first rat to push the other over the edge on to the floor. The egg was unbroken and then both rats proceeded to roll the egg on to the nearby doorway, out into the orchard.'

The farmer went down at once to pick the egg up. He had done this for several days, as eggs are eggs in these days. He said the rats seemed able to roll an egg along pretty fast when they got it on level ground and he had lost the first two by not going down at once to pick them up. He was so interested in the scene that he had done nothing to stop it.

The opium poppy *(Papaver somniferum)* is a native of sunnier climes than ours. However, in England during the Middle Ages its relative the common red poppy *(P. rhoeas)* was considered to be a remedy for pleurisy, ague and various other ailments.

Was this kind of action the answer to the mystery of the egg I had found? Had it been transported by rats which had been disturbed before they could enjoy their booty? I would dearly have liked to be there to see. In nature you sometimes stumble by chance on a strange occurrence; at other times you can watch for hours on end and see nothing.

✳

On a journey across country we went into a pub in Wiltshire. The 'public' was a large L-shaped room with an L-shaped bar at the corner of which was a massive square-sided pillar flanked by fussy little wings. You could hear but not see the few customers on the other side and at first I took no notice of them. Presently, however, they began to raise their voices, there was much scoffing and scepticism against one lone voice which went on protesting.

I pricked up my ears, not in expectation of a quarrel but because of the subject of the conversation. They were talking about trout-tickling – at least one man was while the other three or four were rejecting his claim as sheer fantasy – though in fact they used more colourful terms than that. I could stand it no longer. I went to the support of the hard-pressed champion of an illegal but highly skilled activity. He gratefully acknowledged my help.

'Half a mo'!' he said and shot out of the pub. A few minutes later he returned carrying a pail of water in which swam a fine trout that must have weighed almost a pound. 'There! That's the fellow I was telling you about. Tickled 'un just now afore I came in here! Here!' he turned to me in an excess of gratitude. 'You have 'un! You take him –'

If we had not been travelling, I might have done. As it was it had been sufficient reward to add my pontifications on the art of trout-tickling and reduce the audience to a silence which, if not respectful, was at least a tacit admission that there must be something in it if the old codger said so.

Moorland streams are no use for trout-tickling. The water has got to be comparatively warm, inducing a drowsy contentment in the trout. You wade stealthily into the water – which may be pleasantly balmy to the trout but which even in summertime is tingling cold. You know your river and are aware that the trout is resting under a convenient ledge of the bank.

Carefully you work your hand through the water towards him. Painfully slowly, achingly gently, you grope about until you can feel the smooth, slippery body. You have to be minutely patient, glide your hand along as if it were part of the river; make the slightest twitch and the trout streaks away. Even when the water is almost lapping your ears and your thighs are beginning to knot with cramp, you have to continue your subtle ploy.

Gently, oh so gently you tickle the trout's belly. With the tips of your fingers you stroke it and stroke it, lulling it into a feeling of piscine contentment; you need fingers of swansdown or lamb's-wool. No use hurrying, however cold you are getting. You have to tickle the trout gently, gently, all the time working your hand slowly forward until you can grasp the fish round the middle. No use seizing the trout too far back or too far forward; if you do, he just pops through your fingers like a pea out of a pod.

August

I happen to glance out of the bathroom window while shaving: a small unfamiliar patch of white twenty yards out in the field catches my eye. I peer again: no doubt about it – *they* have begun! Mushrooms! Hurrying on my clothes, I sally forth, basket hopefully in hand, the step springier by thirty years at least. Of all the wild fruits of the earth, blackberries, hazel-nuts, bilberries ('whorts' in Devon), crab-apples, it is mushrooms that evoke the most excitement. Seeking them, gathering them is like finding treasure trove.

Demure, with a peculiar, unmistakable whiteness of their own, they nestle in the grass, sometimes visible a hundred yards away, sometimes obstinately out of sight until you almost kick them from their nesting-place (and oh, the chagrin, at perfectly good mushrooms ruined by clumsy sheep or cattle!). It is no use simply walking straight across a field in search of mushrooms – you must do your mushrooming from several different directions for they are elusive creatures and I am almost persuaded they sometimes bob down out of sight at your approach. In fact, you have to quarter the terrain like an owl quartering for mice.

Their magically rapid growth, their delightful newness, the fact that you go seeking them in the early morning, with the sun swimming in molten gold, the grass heavy with dew, the whole world born afresh, all contribute to the attraction of mushrooming. Something for nothing comes into it, too, and the fact that you go trespassing without the slightest qualms. And of course the anticipation of bacon and mushrooms for breakfast, spiced by the admiration of less matinal members of the household.

All that of course concerns the field mushroom and the horse mushroom, the favourites of the cautious Englishman. But many others are worth knowing, the fat honey-combed cep in the autumn woods, the nutty blusher, the yellow chanterelle with its delicate apricot scent, blewits, and the morels that you find in northern parts. Only a few are truly poisonous, notably the ugly, pallid *Amanita phalloides* or death-cap, and that is a real killer.

But eaten or not, mushrooms, toadstools, fungi, call them what you will, have intrigued and mystified us for many centuries, especially in ancient days before their means of generation, spores floating on the air, was known. Many people thought they were produced by thunder; Pliny believed they originated from mud and the acrid juices of the earth.

✳

I came across a pair of burying beetles busy interring the carcase of a field-vole. Nicknamed sextons because of their activities, these beetles are appropriately sometimes entirely black. This pair, however, was handsomely patched with an almost orange colour. They worked with single-minded intensity, oblivious to the giant from another world looming over them.

Like many beetles, sextons possess an acute sense of smell, derived from organs situated in the feelers or antennae. This enables them to locate animal carcases at considerable distances which are soon covered by their strong flight. A pair of sextons always work in conjunction and on finding the dead mouse, mole or bird, they creep underneath it, dig away industriously so that the carcase sinks and loose soil gradually covers it.

No salvage tug could guard its prize more jealously: if a rival pair of undertakers arrive on the scene, they are fought off ferociously. If the ground is too hard, the sextons drag the carcase a little way off, for in relation to their size they are extremely strong. The burial accomplished, the female lays her eggs in the decomposing flesh which serves as a larder for her grubs when they hatch out.

*

Like most other sports, shooting has become big business. In this case, however, it is the performers who pay for the privilege of taking part and the owners of the *champ de bataille* who benefit. Nowhere is this more evident than in grouse-shooting; enormous sums are paid, by Americans and Europeans, for shooting-rights on the moors of Scotland and Northern England, £300 per day per gun being a perfectly normal tariff. Grouse-shooting is the main income of many a lordly estate and on an average property of, say twenty thousand acres, half will be devoted to the sport.

The opening day of the season is also the greatest day – the so-called 'Glorious Twelfth' of August. But as far as the grouse are concerned, the paths of glory lead if not to the grave only to the gourmet's table. Until put right by my fraternal superiors I used in childhood to be somewhat confused by this exciting title, feeling that it must at least commemorate yet another of our naval victories over the French, similar to the 'Glorious First of June'.

Indeed, the logistics of the occasion were worthy of some military action: before the use of motor-cars and aircraft became common, Euston and King's Cross stations before the Twelfth would be thronged with moustachioed, tweed-clad gentlemen and their ladies, deferential servants, gun-cases, pigskin valises – and guards and attendants on such trains would wax fat on guinea tips. After the great day the same sleek trains would come puffing importantly back, laden with the first of the 'bag', while nowadays aircraft rush it to London where fashionable diners-

The 'Glorious Twelfth'. As Henry Alken pointed out in *The National Sports of Great Britain* (1821): 'The pursuit of moor-game is not to be classed with those gentle exercises which afford gratification without fatigue to the sportsman; on the contrary it is one of the most laborious and fatiguing exertions which can be taken with the gun ...'

out the very same evening regale themselves on grouse – in spite
of the fact that you do not really reckon to eat the bird or any
other game until it has been suitably hung. Or do those grouse
that appear so expeditiously on the menu in reality come out of
the freezer from the previous season?

The fascination of the sport lies partly in the superb *mise-en-
scène* – lonely, spacious, undulating moors, the purple heather
loud with bees, the air charged with the pungent scent of
bog-myrtle, perhaps a golden eagle far off like an eyelash in the
sky, red deer on the distant horizon, the nostalagic cry of the
curlew. But mainly it is the nature of the quarry. Willow grouse,
hazel grouse, black grouse, ptarmigan, the mighty capercaillie,
nicknamed horse-of-the-woods, all belong to the same family

them profitably to a souvenir shop. How many of those who buy them to decorate shelf or arm-chair or, God save us, to hang in the rear window of their car, appreciate their ancient origin?

The making of the corn-dolly was both a celebration of the harvest and a propitiation ceremony. At the cutting of the last sheaf of wheat the reapers gathered up a handful of straw and plaited the ends together, tying them with gaily coloured ribbons if possible. Then they paraded this effigy triumphantly, brandishing their sickles joyfully in what was called in the south-west the ceremony of 'Crying the Neck', neck coming from the Old Norse *nek,* a sheaf. At the same time they chanted:

We-ha-neck! We-ha-neck!
Well a-plowed! Well a-sowed!
We've reaped! And we've a-mowed!
Hurrah! Hurrah! Hurrah!
Well a-cut! Well a-bound!
Well-a-zot upon the ground!
We-ha-neck! We-ha-neck!
Hurrah! Hurrah! Hurrah!

In East Anglia, however, the last stalks of grain were left standing. These were plaited together at the top and bound with ribbons; the reapers then proceeded to hurl their sickles at it from a suitable distance and whoever managed to cut it gained the prize. Eventually this last cut was dressed up, fashioned crudely into a human figure known as the Corn-baby or even Harvest-queen and carried home in triumph. A similar custom existed in Shropshire where the last sheaf was plaited together and known as the gander's neck. When it was finally cut down in the sickle-throwing contest, it was presented to the farmer's wife who kept it as a good luck token until the next harvest.

Perhaps as well as corn-dollies someone should introduce the Harvest-mare to the souvenir market. So much depended on the harvest that it was an occasion for triumph and merriment; another year's sustenance was ensured. Our deep-freeze, super-market generation has no inkling of how closely hunger lurked at the fringes of our forefathers' lives. The last sheaf would be made into a representation of a mare which the workers who had accomplished their reaping would ironically despatch to a neighbouring farm where the work was still going on.

✳

I utterly appreciate Gerard Manley Hopkins's sentiments in *Inversnaid:*

What would the world be, once bereft
Of wet and of wildness? Let them be left,
O let them be left, wildness and wet;
Long live the weeds and the wilderness yet.

A grey seal guarding its pup. In a note to Sir Walter Scott's *Lord of the Isles* it is said that: 'The seal displays a taste for music, which could scarcely be expected from its habits and local predilections. Seals will long follow a boat in which any musical instrument is played, and even a tune simply whistled has attractions for them.'

All the same, back from a holiday in Scotland, I felt a bit aggrieved at the state of the garden. I could also appreciate why the Saxons used to call August 'Weed-month'. My garden-help unavoidably absent, and the docks, handsome and tall as grenadiers, nettles, forgiven perhaps because of their value to butterflies, and goose-grass, so clinging that the Greeks called it Philanthropon because of its 'fondness' for mankind, all rampant on every side, like an army that had lain in ambush.

But at least from that jaunt, unforgettable memories. First, seals – grey or Atlantic seals (the second adjective is more accurate, for the species can vary in colour through black, grey, fawn, dark brown) – brief glimpses, maybe, but sufficient to remind one what magnificent creatures they are: 'strong manbreasted things that stood from the sea, and sent a deep sea voice through all the land.'

There they lay, far below us, basking on the rocks while the lacework of foam lapped nearer all the time. Sleekly glistening, bulky (a grey bull can weigh five hundredweight), they occasionally wriggled and shouldered and jostled for greater comfort. We could not see any babies, it was too early, though it would not be long before they were born: thirty-pound infants that grow with astonishing rapidity nourished on their mother's milk which is the richest known, containing 50 per cent fat; a seal pup puts on four pounds in weight every day during suckling. Ironically, however, in such a marine creature, the young seal cannot swim for almost a month and goes through great distress in the process of learning, being deserted by his mother who breeds again almost immediately. In contrast, the smaller common seal can swim and dive expertly from birth.

Now hunger was stirring the seals – it was not alarm or they would have gone charging off fast. Ponderously, with almost painful effort in their every movement, they heaved themselves across the elephant-grey rocks. Once in the sea they were

Pliny said that toadstools come from mud and the acrid juices of moist earth. Nicander, however, declared that they are formed when the central heat of the globe rarifies the mud of the earth.

transformed, and looking down on those pellucid boreal waters we could see them gliding, twisting, swooping in easy, sculpted grace as they went off on their forays. Sometimes a pair of seals will work a shoal of fish as expertly as gun-dogs working a covey of partridges. They harry the fish to and fro between each other so methodically they might have been trained for the job.

But the 'damage' (damage to whose interests? – not to those of the seals or even of nature!) seals do has always been grossly exaggerated – and a great deal of their food consists of conger eels, lumpsuckers and the like. Man has so greedily plundered the seas near and distant that he constantly seeks for a scapegoat.

Other fishers of the sea were working close by, as magnificent in their own way as the seals. Perhaps three hundred feet above the wrinkled sea, numbers of gannets were floating, admirable in their nonchalant cruising. The 'Solan goose' is one of the most spectacular of fishermen. This striking, ivory-white bird, whose wings span six feet, is the peer even of the eagle and the falcon in its mastery of the air.

Now here they tilted and wheeled, keenly watching for fish worthy of their attention. Then, one after another, with half closed wings, they plunged in a plummeting, glorious dive. Near the surface they closed their pointed wings completely and shot down like feathered barbs in pursuit of their prey, and explosion after explosion of water marked their doomful plunge. Unlike the cormorant, the gannet usually swallows its fish before it emerges from the water.

As I watched those great, goose-sized birds plunging from their lofty stations, I found myself remembering the gruesome story of vengeance exacted in L. A. G. Strong's *The Brothers,* in which one of the characters is tied to a stake in the sea with a herring fastened to his head, whereupon a diving gannet obligingly splits his skull – a unique but somewhat improbable way of having someone murdered!

High summer has indeed arrived when the rosy-purple flowers of the rosebay willow-herb *(Epilobium angustifolium)* appear.

✳

On that same holiday I went to see a falconer friend. In the mews, once a stable, I was introduced to Martia, a peregrine falcon, who sat docile and patient on her master's gauntleted wrist, her head hooded, jesses and leash of kangaroo-skin on her yellow shanks. She was sharp-set, that is she had been fed that day on washed meat, meat soaked in water to spoil it of its juices, and so make her keener on the chase.

When the tufted Dutch hood was taken off her proud eyes were revealed, dark gleaming pools, neither beaten nor nervous, defiant rather. Her carriage, too, was proud and alert, and captivity did not seem to have marred her in any way – until I remembered a trapped wild falcon I once saw, erect and trim, eyes calmly noble, faintly enquiring, and every feather clean-cut and crisp, the bloom of health on it; I realized the difference.

Out on the moor in the sharp, blue afternoon, Martia's collaborator, a setter, whose mild, friendly eyes were in extreme

contrast to hers, ranged the heather. We followed, accompanied by a spaniel, Martia still hooded until the setter should make his point. There were only a few grouse on the moor, a state apparently necessary to the success of game-hawking, for where the prospective quarry is abundant a falcon may be confused and too distracted to stoop at a particular bird.

Methodically the setter ranged and quartered, drawing up to his point after birds which, if there at all, would be creeping away through the heather, refusing to fly as long as possible. Suddenly the plumey tail stiffened, the tip vibrated with momentary uncertainty, then went rigid, and in that position the setter waited faithfully. The hood was struck, the leash removed, and eagerly, with a sweep of the falconer's arm, Martia was sent out in neat, dashing flight. At first it might have seemed that she had no intention of joining in the sport, and was determined to find her own. She circled away far and wide on quick, winnowing wings. This was in order to reach her pitch, towards which she continued to soar, until she looked like a swift curving in the sky.

Meanwhile we circled round the motionless setter until we were some way in front of him, the grouse between him and us. Martia was soaring in wide circles, and I thought of the power of those deep brown eyes staring down upon the heather, waiting for the grouse to be flushed. Presently she ceased to circle so widely and I could see through the glasses that she was cruising leisurely; she was ready. The grouse were put up ridiculously near us; away went the birds, four or five of them, travelling at a great pace. I watched the falcon. She tipped over, head first, and with wings curving back about her tail (or train, to use the parlance of falconry), came falling nearer and nearer at awe-inspiring speed.

She fell behind the grouse she had marked out and, closing in on him in a sharp curve, struck him down. The sound of the impact was like the driving of fist into palm, and was audible fifty or sixty yards away. Brown feathers burst out; the grouse dropped like a stone, but, incredible though it seemed after that terrific blow, he darted out of the heather, sped off down the slope and dived into refuge under some heather-scrag. Now the spaniel's turn came. While Martia waited on expectantly, the spaniel was sent ahead to put up the grouse, which he quickly did. The chase continued; the two birds disappeared down the slope, and by now my sympathies were inevitably with the grouse. I marvelled that any creature could have recovered from the effects of the falcon's devastating stoop.

A few minutes later Martia reappeared, evidently having lost her quarry and prepared to wait on as she had been trained to do – that is, to go ringing up high above the setter until another grouse was flushed. This happened after a long tramp through the heather, during which time the falcon followed the ranging of the setter. Away clattered the grouse. Before they had gone a score of yards, down came the falcon, so close that we heard the

Part of a nesting colony of gannets on Bass Rock in the Firth of Forth showing the dense crowding of adults (pale) and young (dark). For many centuries the men of Ness in the Hebrides made annual expeditions to the islet of Sulisgeir to kill and salt for future sale thousands of 'guga', the immature young of the gannet, whose flesh was considered a luxury.

thrilling swish of her stoop. This time there was no anti-climax to the onslaught. She struck her victim down, the brown feathers dithered out. The stricken grouse collapsed, fell, and literally bounced out of the heather with the force of the blow, then, dropping down, lay still, his brown back ripped open by the hind talon of Martia.

After that exhibition of skill and power, it was surprising to be told that 'she'd done enough for today'. Falconers are jealous of their charges and, however proud of them they may be, they steadfastly refuse excess of showing them off at the risk of future spoiling. When Martia had been tied to a portable weathering-block she was left awhile to enjoy the reward of skill – a meal of grouse.

Falconry is certainly one of the most spectacular examples of Man's partnership with wild creatures. It is usually a sign of an advanced civilization, for falconry is not practised by primitive people. At least three thousand years ago it was an established sport in countries such as Persia and India. In mediaeval England falconry was very much a status symbol. Only the royal or the noble were allowed to keep the falcon, grandest of hunting-birds; the merlin, lovely little 'stone-falcon' of the moors, about the size of a missel-thrush, was considered right for ladies; young men were allotted the hobby, a miniature peregrine which still occasionally comes to the south country in summer.

But impressed though I was with Martia's skill and power and all the patient training my friend had exercised, I still find more natural the marvellous hovering of our local kestrels as they hunt the meadows for field-voles.

✻

Why 'butterflies'? As I lounged drowsily watching the butterflies gathering, floating, flickering, drifting, in all their varied splendour on the purple buddleia whose mealy scent is one of the delights of late summer, I found myself muttering 'Butterflies, why are they called butterflies?' as I remembered wondering in identical terms as a child many years ago: 'they're nothing to do with butter and they aren't flies!'

It isn't only I who am puzzled – nobody knows the origin of the word, not even the learned *Oxford English Dictionary* which, although explaining that it derives from the Old English *buttor-fléoge,* adds dismissively 'the reason for the name is unknown'. In contrast we know the origin of 'buddleia' which perpetuates the memory of one Adam Buddle, who lived in Augustan times and really ought to be the patron saint of butterflies!

Does it matter if we do not know the origin of butterfly? The

Papilio machaon is the only English representative of the swallowtails. These are, however, a large family including the birdwings of south-east Asia. The birdwings are the largest known butterflies with a wing-span of ten inches.

And he thrusts out his fantastic branchy head and roars — they call it belling, though it has no resemblance to the wildest bell ringing out to the wild sky: the word comes from the same stem as bellow. In fact, the sound is like a cross between the grunting cough of a lion and the moaning of a bull. This mournful plaint echoes through the combes — and is heard by other stags who take up the challenge. At times you can hear a dozen stags challenging and counter-challenging, the effect confused by the fact that the animals are constantly on the move.

The most anxious among the stags is the leader of the hinds. The danger to the integrity of his harem comes not only or chiefly from his immediate challenger, but from the hangers-on skulking at the edge of the scene. These stags wait until the two main contenders are confronting each other, and then attempt to sneak in, hoping to split up the herd and drive off some of the hinds. Because the more splendid of the stags are pre-occupied, distracted by hatred of each other, it means that very often the hinds are served by inferior animals. The survival of the fittest does not always apply.

Although several stags may be challenging at the same time, the leader of the herd knows there is really only one other stag who matters, at least for the time being. In a scene of urgent bedlam the two rivals trot closer, awe-inspiring in their animal strength and fury, neck and shoulders bristling with a mantle of coarse hair. One almost expects to see fire and smoke issue from their nostrils instead of their vaporous breath.

Each stag advances again, pauses, groans hollowly, then rushes upon the other. With a furious clattering of antlers they meet and stagger with the shock. Recovering, they fence and strike again with such force one would think to see them stunned or their antlers splintered.

With legs splayed out to keep their balance, they strike again and again, pushing, feinting, their proud necks bowed. They stand hoof to hoof, as it were, and fight it out with grunting intensity, all else forgotten. Time after time there is a violent clattering as each stag tries to pierce his rival with his brow tine — the short tines nearest the head that are the real weapons of the red deer. Their antlers bleed, their dishevelled sides heave, savage noises rise from their swollen throats.

But it does not last long. It *has* been known for the antlers to be locked together when both of the contestants eventually perish, but that is extremely rare. Very soon one or other of the stags knows he is beaten and withdraws, roaring defiance, to avoid further injury. It is highly unusual for wild animals to 'fight to the death'; their motto is rather live to fight another day. The exceptions are perhaps the mole and the shrew, bearing out the adage that the smaller they are the fiercer they come. They can be particularly beastly to each other at mating-time.

As far as the red deer are concerned, it is not only the vanquished who is willing to break off the encounter: the victor

(*ABOVE*) Stubble burning in autumn makes the land look like a battle zone through which a ravaging army has passed.

(*ABOVE, RIGHT*) Swallows gathering together prior to migration. Two hundred years ago men were not at all certain that birds migrated.

Linnaeus believed that swallows hibernated and Gilbert White was only convinced about migration by evidence from his brother who was

(LEFT) The foxglove *(Digitalis purpurea)* has many aliases: dead man's bells, finger-flower, flap dock, witches' bells.

(RIGHT) Ducks always seem to have a much greater sense of enjoyment than hens. They also have a habit of wandering far and near which often leads them into trouble.

throat of a friend of mine who suffered from a septic wound for some time afterwards. Although it is fair to say that the rat was probably not attacking its assailant, but trying to leap over her shoulder as she stooped to hit it. Occasionally, a rat will stand up to a ferret, and when ferrets were muzzled, many a rat made a successful, savage and fatal counter-attack.

The brown rat, which is the one I am concerned with here, only took up residence in Britain about 250 years ago. Being more fecund and aggressive it ousted the so-called 'native' black rat, whose chief claim to fame was as a carrier of the bubonic plague, the 'Black Death' which decimated the human population time after time. ('A dreadful plague in London was, In the year sixty-five, Which swept an hundred thousand souls Away; yet I alive!') The black rat itself, which is smaller and more slender than the brown, probably only reached this country round about the twelfth century; legend has it that it arrived in the ships of returning crusaders. Nowadays it still exists in small numbers in various sea-ports and no doubt is still shipborne.

The brown rat population seems to have irrupted in Central Asia in the late seventeenth and early eighteenth centuries. The naturalist Thomas Pennant estimated the species' arrival in Britain at about 1720, while fervent Jacobites, notably the peerless Charles Waterton, were convinced it accompanied George I and dubbed it the Hanoverian rat. ('It actually came over in the same ship that conveyed the new dynasty to these shores.') The less partisan called it the Norway rat.

There is something disturbing about rats; perhaps it is their furtive skulking ways, their association with dubious haunts such as sewers. In fact the rat is a scrupulously clean animal in the way it grooms itself; it has even been known to groom itself between attacks by a ferret. At times you can sense the presence of rats even though you do not actually see them; at other times their sheer numbers force their attention on you. Once I witnessed a 'rat-flit'. Not far from the Sussex farm where I once worked, there was a slaughterhouse. One night this caught fire. I was walking home at the time and stopped to watch the blaze. To get a better view I climbed on to a cart shed and was thankful to have done so. For presently I became aware of a strangely unnerving sound and looking down was aware of a great number of rats making their way past. I don't know how many there were of them, certainly scores, but it seemed hundreds and I could see their eyes glinting as they hurried on. I stayed a long time after the fire had subsided before venturing down.

Nothing is safe from the rat; it can swim expertly, climb with ease, swarm along telegraph wires, gnaw its way through concrete blocks or lead water-pipes. It is omnivorous: fish, fowl, flesh, vegetable, mollusc, all are equally acceptable; it will cheerfully turn cannibal, too. And it is ubiquitous: on various remote islands, wildlife has been seriously affected by it. But of course it lives most fatly in the presence of Man; it is currently estimated by the United Nations Environment Secretariat that rats consume enough of Man's annual farm-produce to feed 200 million people and that if adequate attention was paid to storing grain the world food outlook would be radically different.

Well, I suppose if I had adequately protected my golden-yellow ducklings...

*

Once long ago as I was walking along a lane, there rang out from the field close by a shrill, wailing scream. It could only have been made by a rabbit being assaulted by a stoat. I clambered over a gate and legged it towards the place the sound had come from.

Immobilized by terror, the rabbit was huddled by the hedge. The stoat, alarmed by my approach, had disappeared. But in a few moments, in the characteristic manner of his kind, he emerged, chakkering resentfully, and only retreated at a near miss from a stick. Before long the rabbit came to again and presently humpled away, safe at least for the time being, while I self-righteously resumed my walk.

I would not interfere like that nowadays. I might hurry towards the spot, but only in the hope of watching the stoat at work, not to save the rabbit. I was reminded of all this early one morning when I sat and watched a hedgehog consuming a frog. A callous attitude on my part? I think not. What right had I to interfere in a natural process? Wild animals hunt only to obtain food; there is no such thing as cruelty in nature. The stoat killing the rabbit, the hedgehog munching the living frog, spider sucking the life-juices of a moth, sparrowhawk striking down a song-bird, all are acting only in the way there were created to act, and death to one creature is life to another. It is a continuing circle, starting – and ending – with the worm. Or, as Emerson's Brahma saw it, it is all a case of

How lizard fed on ant, and snake on him,
And kite on both; and how the fish-hawk robbed
The fish-tiger of that which it had seized;
The shrike chasing the bulbul, which did hunt
The jewelled butterflies; till everywhere
Each slew a slayer and in turn was slain,
Life living upon death.

Only Man is consciously cruel; only Man hunts for sport or profit; only man has wiped out whole orders of bird and beast. No wild predator has ever caused the extinction of a single species.

✳

A mystery: a hen's egg neatly ensconced in a little hollow under the exposed roots of an old appletree. No hen was small enough to have laid there, for the roots grew in the form of a claw under which she could not have crept. Any thieving magpie or crow would have eaten the egg on the spot. In any case, the laying-box was inside the shippon, almost ten yards away. So who or what was responsible?

At once I called to mind stories of rats using hen-houses as a kind of take-away establishment. There is no disputing the fact that rats are capable of removing eggs intact; it is the method which has for long been the subject of argument. Some observers claim that they roll the egg away with their chin or tucked between chin and forepaws. But the favourite story is typified by an account that appeared in *The Zoologist* over a hundred years ago.

The rector of a parish in Westmorland assured me that he
had witnessed this feat. Having lost many eggs belonging
to a laying hen, he was induced to watch to discover the
thief. One morning, soon after the cackling bird had
given warning that she had deposited an egg, he observed
two rats come out of a hole in the hen-house and proceed
direct to the nest. One of the rats then lay down on its
side, while the other rat rolled the egg so near it that it
could embrace it with his feet. Having now obtained a
secure hold on its egg, its companion dragged it into the
hole by its tail, and disappeared.

This prototype tale has been repeated ad infinitum. Unfortunately no reputable and completely reliable naturalist has observed the feat, while the 'witnesses' who have claimed to see it all omit to record how the second rat pulled the transporter-rat along.

The word 'barn' is derived from the Old English *bere-ern*, 'the barley place'. But the Dutch barn (shown on the left in this photograph), which has been widely adopted in this country, is only useful for storing hay or straw. Nothing has ever really taken the place of the traditional barn, shown here on the right partly hidden by trees.

They talk of its standing erect and holding the tail over its shoulder, but presumably not even the Westmorland parson would have suggested that it held the tail in its paws. A recumbent rat would have been a hefty weight for another to haul and the latter's teeth would have exerted a painful grip on the transporter-rat's tail.

In *Animal Legends*, the late Maurice Burton provides a variation on the story. He received it in a letter from a correspondent in Gloucestershire and once again it is at second hand, indeed third hand.

This account was given to me by a mason who was working for a local farmer doing repairs to a barn. The farmer asked him if he would like to see something unusual and took him up to the loft above his stable. 'He bade me be quiet and look down through a knot-hole in the floor, so I did and there was a hen in the manger, sitting wide up in the corner. In a few minutes, up she got clacking like they do and then perched on the manger and flew off. Farmer put up his hand to keep me quiet and in a couple of minutes I could see a rat coming up the post and then another one following him up into the manger. Then they got the egg out of the bit of nest-hay and each of the rats rolled it up on the ledge of the manger by their forepaws helped by their hindlegs. When the egg was

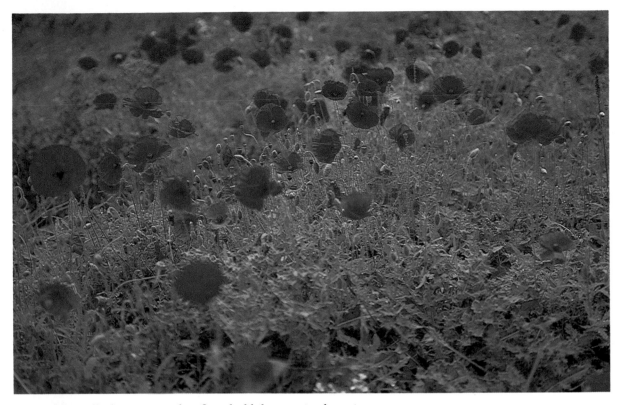

safely rolled up on to this flat shelf they waited a minute, and then one rat lay down on his back and the other rolled the egg on to the one who was lying down. He at once clasped it safely between fore and back paws, where it lay as in a square furry cup. As both rats were on the flat shelf it was quite easy for the first rat to push the other over the edge on to the floor. The egg was unbroken and then both rats proceeded to roll the egg on to the nearby doorway, out into the orchard.'

The farmer went down at once to pick the egg up. He had done this for several days, as eggs are eggs in these days. He said the rats seemed able to roll an egg along pretty fast when they got it on level ground and he had lost the first two by not going down at once to pick them up. He was so interested in the scene that he had done nothing to stop it.

The opium poppy *(Papaver somniferum)* is a native of sunnier climes than ours. However, in England during the Middle Ages its relative the common red poppy *(P. rhoeas)* was considered to be a remedy for pleurisy, ague and various other ailments.

Was this kind of action the answer to the mystery of the egg I had found? Had it been transported by rats which had been disturbed before they could enjoy their booty? I would dearly have liked to be there to see. In nature you sometimes stumble by chance on a strange occurrence; at other times you can watch for hours on end and see nothing.

*

On a journey across country we went into a pub in Wiltshire. The 'public' was a large L-shaped room with an L-shaped bar at the corner of which was a massive square-sided pillar flanked by fussy little wings. You could hear but not see the few customers on the other side and at first I took no notice of them. Presently, however, they began to raise their voices, there was much scoffing and scepticism against one lone voice which went on protesting.

I pricked up my ears, not in expectation of a quarrel but because of the subject of the conversation. They were talking about trout-tickling – at least one man was while the other three or four were rejecting his claim as sheer fantasy – though in fact they used more colourful terms than that. I could stand it no longer. I went to the support of the hard-pressed champion of an illegal but highly skilled activity. He gratefully acknowledged my help.

'Half a mo'!' he said and shot out of the pub. A few minutes later he returned carrying a pail of water in which swam a fine trout that must have weighed almost a pound. 'There! That's the fellow I was telling you about. Tickled 'un just now afore I came in here! Here!' he turned to me in an excess of gratitude. 'You have 'un! You take him – '

If we had not been travelling, I might have done. As it was it had been sufficient reward to add my pontifications on the art of trout-tickling and reduce the audience to a silence which, if not respectful, was at least a tacit admission that there must be something in it if the old codger said so.

Moorland streams are no use for trout-tickling. The water has got to be comparatively warm, inducing a drowsy contentment in the trout. You wade stealthily into the water – which may be pleasantly balmy to the trout but which even in summertime is tingling cold. You know your river and are aware that the trout is resting under a convenient ledge of the bank.

Carefully you work your hand through the water towards him. Painfully slowly, achingly gently, you grope about until you can feel the smooth, slippery body. You have to be minutely patient, glide your hand along as if it were part of the river; make the slightest twitch and the trout streaks away. Even when the water is almost lapping your ears and your thighs are beginning to knot with cramp, you have to continue your subtle ploy.

Gently, oh so gently you tickle the trout's belly. With the tips of your fingers you stroke it and stroke it, lulling it into a feeling of piscine contentment; you need fingers of swansdown or lamb's-wool. No use hurrying, however cold you are getting. You have to tickle the trout gently, gently, all the time working your hand slowly forward until you can grasp the fish round the middle. No use seizing the trout too far back or too far forward; if you do, he just pops through your fingers like a pea out of a pod.

August

I happen to glance out of the bathroom window while shaving: a small unfamiliar patch of white twenty yards out in the field catches my eye. I peer again: no doubt about it – *they* have begun! Mushrooms! Hurrying on my clothes, I sally forth, basket hopefully in hand, the step springier by thirty years at least. Of all the wild fruits of the earth, blackberries, hazel-nuts, bilberries ('whorts' in Devon), crab-apples, it is mushrooms that evoke the most excitement. Seeking them, gathering them is like finding treasure trove.

Demure, with a peculiar, unmistakable whiteness of their own, they nestle in the grass, sometimes visible a hundred yards away, sometimes obstinately out of sight until you almost kick them from their nesting-place (and oh, the chagrin, at perfectly good mushrooms ruined by clumsy sheep or cattle!). It is no use simply walking straight across a field in search of mushrooms – you must do your mushrooming from several different directions for they are elusive creatures and I am almost persuaded they sometimes bob down out of sight at your approach. In fact, you have to quarter the terrain like an owl quartering for mice.

Their magically rapid growth, their delightful newness, the fact that you go seeking them in the early morning, with the sun swimming in molten gold, the grass heavy with dew, the whole world born afresh, all contribute to the attraction of mushrooming. Something for nothing comes into it, too, and the fact that you go trespassing without the slightest qualms. And of course the anticipation of bacon and mushrooms for breakfast, spiced by the admiration of less matinal members of the household.

All that of course concerns the field mushroom and the horse mushroom, the favourites of the cautious Englishman. But many others are worth knowing, the fat honey-combed cep in the autumn woods, the nutty blusher, the yellow chanterelle with its delicate apricot scent, blewits, and the morels that you find in northern parts. Only a few are truly poisonous, notably the ugly, pallid *Amanita phalloides* or death-cap, and that is a real killer.

But eaten or not, mushrooms, toadstools, fungi, call them what you will, have intrigued and mystified us for many centuries, especially in ancient days before their means of generation, spores floating on the air, was known. Many people thought they were produced by thunder; Pliny believed they originated from mud and the acrid juices of the earth.

✳

I came across a pair of burying beetles busy interring the carcase of a field-vole. Nicknamed sextons because of their activities, these beetles are appropriately sometimes entirely black. This pair, however, was handsomely patched with an almost orange colour. They worked with single-minded intensity, oblivious to the giant from another world looming over them.

Like many beetles, sextons possess an acute sense of smell, derived from organs situated in the feelers or antennae. This enables them to locate animal carcases at considerable distances which are soon covered by their strong flight. A pair of sextons always work in conjunction and on finding the dead mouse, mole or bird, they creep underneath it, dig away industriously so that the carcase sinks and loose soil gradually covers it.

No salvage tug could guard its prize more jealously: if a rival pair of undertakers arrive on the scene, they are fought off ferociously. If the ground is too hard, the sextons drag the carcase a little way off, for in relation to their size they are extremely strong. The burial accomplished, the female lays her eggs in the decomposing flesh which serves as a larder for her grubs when they hatch out.

*

Like most other sports, shooting has become big business. In this case, however, it is the performers who pay for the privilege of taking part and the owners of the *champ de bataille* who benefit. Nowhere is this more evident than in grouse-shooting; enormous sums are paid, by Americans and Europeans, for shooting-rights on the moors of Scotland and Northern England, £300 per day per gun being a perfectly normal tariff. Grouse-shooting is the main income of many a lordly estate and on an average property of, say twenty thousand acres, half will be devoted to the sport.

The opening day of the season is also the greatest day – the so-called 'Glorious Twelfth' of August. But as far as the grouse are concerned, the paths of glory lead if not to the grave only to the gourmet's table. Until put right by my fraternal superiors I used in childhood to be somewhat confused by this exciting title, feeling that it must at least commemorate yet another of our naval victories over the French, similar to the 'Glorious First of June'.

Indeed, the logistics of the occasion were worthy of some military action: before the use of motor-cars and aircraft became common, Euston and King's Cross stations before the Twelfth would be thronged with moustachioed, tweed-clad gentlemen and their ladies, deferential servants, gun-cases, pigskin valises – and guards and attendants on such trains would wax fat on guinea tips. After the great day the same sleek trains would come puffing importantly back, laden with the first of the 'bag', while nowadays aircraft rush it to London where fashionable diners-

The 'Glorious Twelfth'. As Henry Alken pointed out in *The National Sports of Great Britain* (1821): 'The pursuit of moor-game is not to be classed with those gentle exercises which afford gratification without fatigue to the sportsman; on the contrary it is one of the most laborious and fatiguing exertions which can be taken with the gun . . .'

out the very same evening regale themselves on grouse – in spite of the fact that you do not really reckon to eat the bird or any other game until it has been suitably hung. Or do those grouse that appear so expeditiously on the menu in reality come out of the freezer from the previous season?

The fascination of the sport lies partly in the superb *mise-en-scène* – lonely, spacious, undulating moors, the purple heather loud with bees, the air charged with the pungent scent of bog-myrtle, perhaps a golden eagle far off like an eyelash in the sky, red deer on the distant horizon, the nostalagic cry of the curlew. But mainly it is the nature of the quarry. Willow grouse, hazel grouse, black grouse, ptarmigan, the mighty capercaillie, nicknamed horse-of-the-woods, all belong to the same family and occur in much of northern Europe, the last three in Britain as well. But the handsome, chunky, chestnut-red *Lagopus scoticus,* with its striking vermilion wattles or comb, its evocative, clattering shout of *go-back, go-back,* occurs only in the British Isles, chiefly in northern parts, though a few introduced birds still survive on Exmoor and Dartmoor.

The grouse flourishes only on moorland, for its principal food is heather, the common ling, of which it eats the green shoots, the flowers and the seed-heads. But it will also feed on the leaves, fruit and buds of many other plants, such as the cranberry, blueberry, even cotton-grass, sweet gale, creeping willow.

In addition to the wild charm of its habitat, the red grouse is the most 'sporting' of birds, as the aficionados term it. In other words it is more difficult to kill because of its speed and variability of flight – unlike, for instance, the blundering pheasant which is always reluctant to take wing. Driven by platoons of flag-waving beaters, the packs of grouse, alternately whirring and gliding and swerving, come over explosively fast and the moorland echoes with a fusillade of shots as the sportsmen in their butts – little bunkers built of turf-sods and stones – go into action like a Home Guard repelling invaders.

It was the railways that invented grouse-shooting as a fashionable sport and indeed turned the Scottish Highlands into a sportsman's paradise – with deer-stalking and salmon-fishing its other glamorous pursuits. Until then the highlands were known only to people like Charles St John who went there to live, or the fanatical Colonel Peter Hawker. But with the coming of the railways the laborious coach journey (from London to Edinburgh alone took many days) became a thing of the past and Scotland was suddenly accessible to southern gentlemen. Moreover, this roughly coincided in 1853 with the introduction by a London gunsmith of the first breech-loader.

Until that time sheep had been the chief source of a highland landlord's income. But landlords discovered they could make more money out of the shooting-rights than out of grazing. Half a century before, the crofters had made way for the sheep; now the sheep were ousted by sporting interests. These in turn are at the mercy of nature; sometimes after bad winters and late springs there is not enough heather to support the artificially stimulated grouse-population, for in the past the bird's natural predators, foxes, eagles, hawks, ravens, hoodie crows, black-backed gulls, even wild cats, were slaughtered wholesale so that the Twelfth could be more glorious still. In some years, notably 1979, this has even caused the opening of the season to be postponed by a matter of weeks.

*

Corn-dollies have become fashionable in recent years. An old woman near here makes marvellously elaborate ones and sells

(ABOVE) Harvest-time in the Lincoln Wolds. 'The harvest truly is plenteous,' said St Matthew, 'but the labourers are few.' This is certainly so in the days of the combine harvester.

(LEFT) A close cousin of the red grouse, the blackcock (Cyrurus tetrix) is at its most spectacular when 'lekking' — performing its peculiar courtship display. It dances like a mad creature with all its glossy plumage and its lyre-shaped tail spread. At this time the moor rings with its hoarse challenges.

them profitably to a souvenir shop. How many of those who buy them to decorate shelf or arm-chair or, God save us, to hang in the rear window of their car, appreciate their ancient origin?

The making of the corn-dolly was both a celebration of the harvest and a propitiation ceremony. At the cutting of the last sheaf of wheat the reapers gathered up a handful of straw and plaited the ends together, tying them with gaily coloured ribbons if possible. Then they paraded this effigy triumphantly, brandishing their sickles joyfully in what was called in the south-west the ceremony of 'Crying the Neck', neck coming from the Old Norse *nek,* a sheaf. At the same time they chanted:

> *We-ha-neck! We-ha-neck!*
> *Well a-plowed! Well a-sowed!*
> *We've reaped! And we've a-mowed!*
> *Hurrah! Hurrah! Hurrah!*
> *Well a-cut! Well a-bound!*
> *Well-a-zot upon the ground!*
> *We-ha-neck! We-ha-neck!*
> *Hurrah! Hurrah! Hurrah!*

In East Anglia, however, the last stalks of grain were left standing. These were plaited together at the top and bound with ribbons; the reapers then proceeded to hurl their sickles at it from a suitable distance and whoever managed to cut it gained the prize. Eventually this last cut was dressed up, fashioned crudely into a human figure known as the Corn-baby or even Harvest-queen and carried home in triumph. A similar custom existed in Shropshire where the last sheaf was plaited together and known as the gander's neck. When it was finally cut down in the sickle-throwing contest, it was presented to the farmer's wife who kept it as a good luck token until the next harvest.

Perhaps as well as corn-dollies someone should introduce the Harvest-mare to the souvenir market. So much depended on the harvest that it was an occasion for triumph and merriment; another year's sustenance was ensured. Our deep-freeze, supermarket generation has no inkling of how closely hunger lurked at the fringes of our forefathers' lives. The last sheaf would be made into a representation of a mare which the workers who had accomplished their reaping would ironically despatch to a neighbouring farm where the work was still going on.

✲

I utterly appreciate Gerard Manley Hopkins's sentiments in *Inversnaid:*

> *What would the world be, once bereft*
> *Of wet and of wildness? Let them be left,*
> *O let them be left, wildness and wet;*
> *Long live the weeds and the wilderness yet.*

A grey seal guarding its pup. In a note to Sir Walter Scott's *Lord of the Isles* it is said that: 'The seal displays a taste for music, which could scarcely be expected from its habits and local predilections. Seals will long follow a boat in which any musical instrument is played, and even a tune simply whistled has attractions for them.'

All the same, back from a holiday in Scotland, I felt a bit aggrieved at the state of the garden. I could also appreciate why the Saxons used to call August 'Weed-month'. My garden-help unavoidably absent, and the docks, handsome and tall as grenadiers, nettles, forgiven perhaps because of their value to butterflies, and goose-grass, so clinging that the Greeks called it Philanthropon because of its 'fondness' for mankind, all rampant on every side, like an army that had lain in ambush.

But at least from that jaunt, unforgettable memories. First, seals — grey or Atlantic seals (the second adjective is more accurate, for the species can vary in colour through black, grey, fawn, dark brown) — brief glimpses, maybe, but sufficient to remind one what magnificent creatures they are: 'strong man-breasted things that stood from the sea, and sent a deep sea voice through all the land.'

There they lay, far below us, basking on the rocks while the lacework of foam lapped nearer all the time. Sleekly glistening, bulky (a grey bull can weigh five hundredweight), they occasionally wriggled and shouldered and jostled for greater comfort. We could not see any babies, it was too early, though it would not be long before they were born: thirty-pound infants that grow with astonishing rapidity nourished on their mother's milk which is the richest known, containing 50 per cent fat; a seal pup puts on four pounds in weight every day during suckling. Ironically, however, in such a marine creature, the young seal cannot swim for almost a month and goes through great distress in the process of learning, being deserted by his mother who breeds again almost immediately. In contrast, the smaller common seal can swim and dive expertly from birth.

Now hunger was stirring the seals — it was not alarm or they would have gone charging off fast. Ponderously, with almost painful effort in their every movement, they heaved themselves across the elephant-grey rocks. Once in the sea they were

Pliny said that toadstools come from mud and the acrid juices of moist earth. Nicander, however, declared that they are formed when the central heat of the globe rarifies the mud of the earth.

transformed, and looking down on those pellucid boreal waters we could see them gliding, twisting, swooping in easy, sculpted grace as they went off on their forays. Sometimes a pair of seals will work a shoal of fish as expertly as gun-dogs working a covey of partridges. They harry the fish to and fro between each other so methodically they might have been trained for the job.

But the 'damage' (damage to whose interests? – not to those of the seals or even of nature!) seals do has always been grossly exaggerated – and a great deal of their food consists of conger eels, lumpsuckers and the like. Man has so greedily plundered the seas near and distant that he constantly seeks for a scapegoat.

Other fishers of the sea were working close by, as magnificent in their own way as the seals. Perhaps three hundred feet above the wrinkled sea, numbers of gannets were floating, admirable in their nonchalant cruising. The 'Solan goose' is one of the most spectacular of fishermen. This striking, ivory-white bird, whose wings span six feet, is the peer even of the eagle and the falcon in its mastery of the air.

Now here they tilted and wheeled, keenly watching for fish worthy of their attention. Then, one after another, with half closed wings, they plunged in a plummeting, glorious dive. Near the surface they closed their pointed wings completely and shot down like feathered barbs in pursuit of their prey, and explosion after explosion of water marked their doomful plunge. Unlike the cormorant, the gannet usually swallows its fish before it emerges from the water.

As I watched those great, goose-sized birds plunging from their lofty stations, I found myself remembering the gruesome story of vengeance exacted in L. A. G. Strong's *The Brothers,* in which one of the characters is tied to a stake in the sea with a herring fastened to his head, whereupon a diving gannet obligingly splits his skull – a unique but somewhat improbable way of having someone murdered!

High summer has indeed arrived when the rosy-purple flowers of the rosebay willow-herb *(Epilobium angustifolium)* appear.

*

On that same holiday I went to see a falconer friend. In the mews, once a stable, I was introduced to Martia, a peregrine falcon, who sat docile and patient on her master's gauntleted wrist, her head hooded, jesses and leash of kangaroo-skin on her yellow shanks. She was sharp-set, that is she had been fed that day on washed meat, meat soaked in water to spoil it of its juices, and so make her keener on the chase.

When the tufted Dutch hood was taken off her proud eyes were revealed, dark gleaming pools, neither beaten nor nervous, defiant rather. Her carriage, too, was proud and alert, and captivity did not seem to have marred her in any way – until I remembered a trapped wild falcon I once saw, erect and trim, eyes calmly noble, faintly enquiring, and every feather clean-cut and crisp, the bloom of health on it; I realized the difference.

Out on the moor in the sharp, blue afternoon, Martia's collaborator, a setter, whose mild, friendly eyes were in extreme

contrast to hers, ranged the heather. We followed, accompanied by a spaniel, Martia still hooded until the setter should make his point. There were only a few grouse on the moor, a state apparently necessary to the success of game-hawking, for where the prospective quarry is abundant a falcon may be confused and too distracted to stoop at a particular bird.

Methodically the setter ranged and quartered, drawing up to his point after birds which, if there at all, would be creeping away through the heather, refusing to fly as long as possible. Suddenly the plumey tail stiffened, the tip vibrated with momentary uncertainty, then went rigid, and in that position the setter waited faithfully. The hood was struck, the leash removed, and eagerly, with a sweep of the falconer's arm, Martia was sent out in neat, dashing flight. At first it might have seemed that she had no intention of joining in the sport, and was determined to find her own. She circled away far and wide on quick, winnowing wings. This was in order to reach her pitch, towards which she continued to soar, until she looked like a swift curving in the sky.

Meanwhile we circled round the motionless setter until we were some way in front of him, the grouse between him and us. Martia was soaring in wide circles, and I thought of the power of those deep brown eyes staring down upon the heather, waiting for the grouse to be flushed. Presently she ceased to circle so widely and I could see through the glasses that she was cruising leisurely; she was ready. The grouse were put up ridiculously near us; away went the birds, four or five of them, travelling at a great pace. I watched the falcon. She tipped over, head first, and with wings curving back about her tail (or train, to use the parlance of falconry), came falling nearer and nearer at awe-inspiring speed.

She fell behind the grouse she had marked out and, closing in on him in a sharp curve, struck him down. The sound of the impact was like the driving of fist into palm, and was audible fifty or sixty yards away. Brown feathers burst out; the grouse dropped like a stone, but, incredible though it seemed after that terrific blow, he darted out of the heather, sped off down the slope and dived into refuge under some heather-scrag. Now the spaniel's turn came. While Martia waited on expectantly, the spaniel was sent ahead to put up the grouse, which he quickly did. The chase continued; the two birds disappeared down the slope, and by now my sympathies were inevitably with the grouse. I marvelled that any creature could have recovered from the effects of the falcon's devastating stoop.

A few minutes later Martia reappeared, evidently having lost her quarry and prepared to wait on as she had been trained to do – that is, to go ringing up high above the setter until another grouse was flushed. This happened after a long tramp through the heather, during which time the falcon followed the ranging of the setter. Away clattered the grouse. Before they had gone a score of yards, down came the falcon, so close that we heard the

Part of a nesting colony of gannets on Bass Rock in the Firth of Forth showing the dense crowding of adults (pale) and young (dark). For many centuries the men of Ness in the Hebrides made annual expeditions to the islet of Sulisgeir to kill and salt for future sale thousands of 'guga', the immature young of the gannet, whose flesh was considered a luxury.

thrilling swish of her stoop. This time there was no anti-climax to the onslaught. She struck her victim down, the brown feathers dithered out. The stricken grouse collapsed, fell, and literally bounced out of the heather with the force of the blow, then, dropping down, lay still, his brown back ripped open by the hind talon of Martia.

After that exhibition of skill and power, it was surprising to be told that 'she'd done enough for today'. Falconers are jealous of their charges and, however proud of them they may be, they steadfastly refuse excess of showing them off at the risk of future spoiling. When Martia had been tied to a portable weathering-block she was left awhile to enjoy the reward of skill – a meal of grouse.

Falconry is certainly one of the most spectacular examples of Man's partnership with wild creatures. It is usually a sign of an advanced civilization, for falconry is not practised by primitive people. At least three thousand years ago it was an established sport in countries such as Persia and India. In mediaeval England falconry was very much a status symbol. Only the royal or the noble were allowed to keep the falcon, grandest of hunting-birds; the merlin, lovely little 'stone-falcon' of the moors, about the size of a missel-thrush, was considered right for ladies; young men were allotted the hobby, a miniature peregrine which still occasionally comes to the south country in summer.

But impressed though I was with Martia's skill and power and all the patient training my friend had exercised, I still find more natural the marvellous hovering of our local kestrels as they hunt the meadows for field-voles.

*

Why 'butterflies'? As I lounged drowsily watching the butterflies gathering, floating, flickering, drifting, in all their varied splendour on the purple buddleia whose mealy scent is one of the delights of late summer, I found myself muttering 'Butterflies, why are they called butterflies?' as I remembered wondering in identical terms as a child many years ago: 'they're nothing to do with butter and they aren't flies!'

It isn't only I who am puzzled – nobody knows the origin of the word, not even the learned *Oxford English Dictionary* which, although explaining that it derives from the Old English *buttor-fléoge,* adds dismissively 'the reason for the name is unknown'. In contrast we know the origin of 'buddleia' which perpetuates the memory of one Adam Buddle, who lived in Augustan times and really ought to be the patron saint of butterflies!

Does it matter if we do not know the origin of butterfly? The

Papilio machaon is the only English representative of the swallowtails. These are, however, a large family including the birdwings of south-east Asia. The birdwings are the largest known butterflies with a wing-span of ten inches.

A lobster moth caterpillar on a beech twig. Nature protects her children in many ways. This caterpillar is a daunting figure and in addition it is able to defend itself by emitting formic acid.

red admiral with its superb, arresting black and scarlet and white, the peacock with its velvety 'eyes', the comma with its jagged edges cut out as it were by divine pinking scissors, the painted lady, fragile migrant from Africa – none would be less beautiful if we did not know their names, or more so because we knew they endured such names as *Inachis io* or *Vanessa atalanta*.

But what used to astonish me as much as this delicate, magic beauty, and still does astonish me, is the contrast between the various stages in this insect's life: the egg, one of several hundred or more, the often hairy or repellent caterpillar, the silken cocoon in which for months on end, sometimes a whole year, the pupa sleeps its way towards perfection, the breaking open of the seemingly varnished chrysalis, and the incredible transformation scene when, lo, the imago comes forth with wings which dry, swell, and presently decorate the air.

Anxiously every summer we look to see how many butterflies there will be. One, alas, that we shall not see again in this country is the large blue which has been officially declared 'probably extinct' by the Nature Conservancy. Quite apart from 'Man's inhumanity to man' which 'makes countless thousands mourn', how can we call ourselves civilized when we never cease destroying the inimitable marvels of nature, from the tiny arion to the supple beauty of the otter which is in danger of going the same way? No word, however measured, no film however vivid, no brush stroke however inspired, can replace them.

September

———◆◆◆———

Very often when sitting at a certain spot on the bank of the river, or rather a little backwater of it, I can be sure of seeing a watershrew at work – and also as he takes his leisure. He has a favourite stone on which to sun himself only a couple of yards away from where an enormously bigger, two-legged mammal also sits enjoying the mellow warmth!

Although little more than three inches in length, discounting his tail, the water-shrew is still rather bigger than the other shrews, and also much darker in colour. In fact this one is almost black, with a white underside. Before long his trunklike snout begins to twitch; he goes trickling swiftly down the bank, with an almost quicksilver movement, to another favourite stone. This is his diving-board and from it he takes a little header into the stream. At once he assumes a beautiful aspect, for in his dense, velvety fur there are pockets of air which give him a silvery appearance – and increase his buoyancy. He is also equipped with delicate swimming-aids consisting of a 'keel' of stiff hairs on the underside of his tail and a similar fringe on the side of each hind foot for better paddling.

Once you know the haunts of a water-shrew it is not difficult to keep watch on him; his range is very limited, while his eyesight is poor. Even when you cannot see him under water, you can often follow his progress by means of the chain of air-bubbles. Like his frequent riverside companion, the rotund, bouncy dipper (alias water-ousel, water-crow, colley, bobby) he seems to have the knack of walking on the bottom by somehow gripping with his feet as he hunts for all sorts of prey, crustaceans, insects, even small frogs and fish-fry.

In common with his relations, the water-shrew is a pugnacious little beast, but in addition he possesses a most peculiar attribute for a mammal. The shrews in general have always had a strange reputation in folklore. One of the most notorious examples of this was in connection with the disease cattle-murrain; an often-attempted cure was to rub the afflicted animals with the leaves and twigs of an ash-tree in a hole in which a live shrew had been incarcerated. Edward Topsell (*c.*1600) described the shrew as 'a ravening beast, feigning itself gentle and tame, but, being touched, it biteth deep, and poisoneth deadly.'

For a long time, this sort of thing was looked upon as an old wives' tale, but modern research has proved that shrews do

(ABOVE) In autumn particularly, the water-shrew wanders a long way from water and sometimes enters houses. It has been known to travel as far as two miles from water.

(ABOVE, RIGHT) A ploughing-match in Surrey. Before the tractor ousted the horse, the annual ploughing-match was an important event – almost a ritual. The invention of the plough had far greater significance for the course of human history than any epoch-making invasion or dynastic upset.

indeed possess a toxic secretion in their salivary glands which can paralyse worms and snails and, if administered in sufficient quantity, can even kill mice. Perhaps shrews need such an aid, for small though they are, they can succumb rapidly to starvation – as they do to shock, which explains the frequent uninjured shrew-corpses one comes across.

In nice contrast to its sinister family reputation, Grant Watson in his *The Common Earth* reveals a very different facet of the water-shrew's character:

> *... my little shrew began to sing. And this was a song, it could not be called mere squeaking. It was well sustained, with a cadence of its own, repeated several times. This shrew-song was about the same length as the simple roundelay of a chaffinch, but the repetition was not so regular, and very faint and shrill. I watched and listened, very pleased that I was given this opportunity of confirming an earlier experience. Yes, unmistakably the sounds came from the shrew, and, as unmistakably as any bird's song, this was a song of happiness and thanksgiving for the return of spring. Sometimes the notes were so faint that I could scarcely hear them, at others there was a peculiar mouse-like squeak, and at others a sound like the gentle sliding of silver coins one over another.*

Well, *my* water-shrew did not sing for me. But as he swam back towards the bank he made a sudden troutlike jump on the surface, maybe he was jumping for joy after being well fed, but more likely he was making a pass at a flying insect. Then he drew

himself out and sat on his diving-stone busily cleaning his fur which looked completely dry after his submersion.

✳

One night while I was visiting friends in Somerset, Blackie the newly-acquired kitten went missing, without leave at that. It could be said of its small owner that, like Tennyson's Mariana,

> *Her tears fell with the dews at even;*
> *Her tears fell ere the dews were dried.*

I volunteered to go out with her and search for the kitten by torchlight. Walking, swishing, through the dew-soaked grass, hopefully calling, hopefully flashing the torch here and there, suddenly a gasp of horror. 'A snake! Look! A great big slimy snake...'

It wasn't. It was an eel.

'But an eel's a fish, isn't it! It can't travel on land!'

It can and does. That eel was on the first stage of its immensely long migration. It was an uphill task, convincing one small girl of that. And after all, for many hundreds of years men were mystified by the creature, particularly its breeding habits. It used to be thought that eels were engendered by earthworms – and that *they* were born of the soil; or that eels, being neither masculine nor feminine, reproduced themselves by rubbing off pieces of skin which became baby eels.

It was not until the present century that the facts about the eel's life cycle became known, thanks largely to the Danish scientist Johannes Schmidt. He helped to solve what was one of

No obstacle is allowed to impede the eel's migrating urge. Here one travels overland. Aristotle declared that eels were engendered by earthworms and that they in turn were born of the soil. Pliny's opinion was that eels, being neither masculine nor feminine, reproduced themselves by rubbing off pieces of skin, which became baby eels.

A Scots pine *(Pinus sylvestris)* being felled in the New Forest. With the coming of the power-saw the woods began to fall at an ever-increasing rate.

the most intriguing marine mysteries by identifying the spawning grounds of the eel as a small area in the western Atlantic – popularly in the region of the sinister Sargasso Sea, where the eels found the great depths necessary for their spawning.

The mystery had all along been heightened by the belief that there existed two distinct species of common eel, the 'yellow' eel and the 'silver' eel. The truth is that the familiar dull yellowish eel, after spending anything from seven to fifteen years in freshwater, suddenly begins to change into its silvery breeding dress which makes it seem a different kind, especially as its eyes grow larger and its snout grows more pointed.

Another change that takes place is that yellow eels are voracious omnivores, eating worms, crayfish, carrion, even frogs and water-voles in the case of the bigger fish but silver eels do not feed at all. Nothing matters now but obedience to the urge that seizes them; the fact that many of them have spent the greater part of their lives in landlocked waters is no obstacle. To reach the nearest river that will take them to the ocean, they travel along ditches, even overland when necessary, wriggling their way at night through the grass, preferably when this is moist from dew or rain.

The three or four thousand mile journey across the Atlantic takes the European eel six months. It is their last journey, for after mating they die, Nature having no more use for them. But each pair of eels have left behind them many million, sometimes up to twenty million, fertilized eggs, though only a tiny proportion of these even hatch. Of those that do, the resulting larvae bear no resemblance to their parents. Flat and about a quarter of an inch in length, they resemble nothing so much as long ribbony leaves tapering from a broad base to a tiny head equipped with needlelike teeth, and they are so transparent that all their internal structure is visible.

Growing bigger all the time, up to about three inches, they remain in the larval stage for two and a half years, finding their way eastward across the Atlantic. A metamorphosis now takes place, to prepare them for their freshwater life. They no longer feed; their larval teeth disappear and are replaced by others. Their flat leaflike shape gives way to a round, slender one and they become miniature eels, or elvers, though for the time being they remain transparent. And in their countless millions they begin to swarm up the rivers of Europe, regardless of any obstacle, and using drains or water-pipes when necessary.

In the years of their adulthood, these minuscule creatures can grow to considerable size. The females sometimes reach four or five feet and a weight of fifteen pounds, the males half that. The eel has for long been esteemed as food. As late as the reign of James I, rents in the Fenland were still being paid in terms of so many thousands of eels. But as Dr Johnson remarked, it is all a question of taste. 'That which is selected as delicate by one country is by its neighbours abhorred as loathsome.'

Oh, by the way, we did find Blackie all right. He had not been devoured by some dastardly eel. In fact, he looked so fat and contented, it might have been the other way round.

*

A mile away from here in a steep, wooded coign of the moor there is a badger sett. It has existed for many years – and many times I have watched a flat-browed black and white striped head waver up out of one of the tunnels and a silvery grey, sturdy body squatting there, as a badger surveyed the prospects, listened, tested the air, and eventually decided it was safe to emerge on its nocturnal round.

Potato-picking in Devon. It is thought that Sir Walter Raleigh first brought the potato from the Americas, planting it on his Irish estates. Mangolds or mangel-wurzels (there is a crop on the right of the photograph) were introduced during the eighteenth century by such progressive farmers as 'Turnip' Townshend and Coke of Norfolk.

I have watched the badgers amble out and stretch up to scrape their claws against a nearby tree, I have watched them gather bundles of dead bracken for bedding and drag it into the sett. I have watched their cubs tussle and romp in mock-fights — during which they once nearly blundered against my feet, so close did they come. For with patience and woodcraft and a favourable wind, you can get some surprisingly intimate glimpses of the badger.

Now the fate of those badgers is at stake, and indeed before this is printed it may have been settled by the men from the Ministry — the Ministry of Agriculture. They have decided in recent years that the badger is a menace to cattle-farming because it *may* be a carrier of bovine tuberculosis. Not, mark you, badger tuberculosis. It is the cows that sometimes have the disease,

neighbouring badgers *may,* claim the men from the Ministry, pick it up and subsequently re-infect other cattle.

The Ministry admit they cannot tell if badgers have the disease until a carcase is examined. So, to be on the safe side, the perpetual motto of Whitehall, they are slaughtering the badgers en masse, healthy and allegedly infected alike. So far in the West Country they have gassed more than ten thousand badgers, and gassing, far from being humane, means that animals choke to death, suffer from convulsions, heart attacks and in general endure a painful and far from instantaneous end.

Why can't cattle be immunised by injection, which is often done in other countries? In any case, all milk is pasteurised or from accredited herds, so there is an infinitesimal danger of human beings catching tuberculosis from it. Indeed, can the

The horses that were hunted by primitive Man were probably the size of these New Forest ponies. Many centuries of selection and breeding were necessary before, for example, a fourteen-hand horse was developed.

A badger grooming itself. The badger's obsession with cleanliness could account for a remarkable badger funeral that Brian Vesey-Fitzgerald recorded. He watched two badgers drag the carcase of another badger from the sett and bury it in a 'grave' that had been dug beforehand. This action may have been prompted by a natural wish to rid their home of a decomposing body.

Ministry state how many people have? It is very odd how certain characters have a phobia about the badger. It brings out the worst in them. Before the war I witnessed some horrific scenes in connection with badger-digging, including dogs subsequently being allowed to bait an animal. (Quote from a classic textbook on terriers and badger-digging: 'I *do* like a badger-dig, the old badger is such a sportsman.') I wrote it all up in a story for the *Cornhill Magazine* and later included it in my first book, *Between the Two Twilights,* which John Murray published – it's out of print, so this isn't a puff. One of the reviews it received was by the editor of a well-known sporting magazine. If what I described was true, he said, it should not have been written about. Now a surrogate badger-dig seems to be taking place in the shape of this gassing campaign. (Unhappily, aside from this official action, badger-digging, with its concomitant brutalities, still goes on, often at night.) Yet the evidence so far adduced to justify the extermination policy certainly does not seem scientifically conclusive. A line of least resistance has been adopted. However, at least the Ministry shows signs of heeding the unease felt by many people and has appointed Lord Zuckerman to head an enquiry into its policy. Its findings will be read with concern.

In the words of Howard Lancum, himself one of the most knowledgeable and sympathetic experts ever employed by the Ministry of Agriculture, 'No other British animal has been subject to so much ill-informed, adverse comment as the badger,

backed by so little evidence.' And that was in a Ministry bulletin, *Wild Mammals and the Land.*

John Clare describes a badger hunt:

He tries to reach the woods a awkward race
But sticks and cudgels quickly stop the chace
He turns agen and drives the noisey crowd
And beats the many dogs in noises loud
He drives away and beats them every one
And then they loose them all and set them on
He falls as dead and kicked by boys and men
Then starts and grins and drives the crowd agen
Till kicked and torn and beaten out he lies
And leaves his hold and cackles groans and dies.

*

(ABOVE) Sheepdogs at a hill farm on the Derbyshire/Cheshire border. Not all experts subscribe to the theory of the dog's origins discussed in the text. F. E. Zeuner, the great authority on domesticated animals, feels that the Indian wolf is a more suitable candidate than the jackal for the role of the dog's ancestor.

(ABOVE, LEFT) Sheepdog trials are held during the autumn. These events provide Man's 'oldest friend' with an opportunity to demonstrate to the world how far he has sublimated the hunting instincts of his ancestors.

I am thrilled, these September mornings, to see the fields strewn with sheets of gossamer. As Thomas Hood wrote about autumn

Shaking his languid locks all dewy bright
With tangled gossamer that fell by night,
Pearling his coronet of golden corn.

Unlike White a generation before him, Hood had no doubts about migration among birds, for he remarks that 'the swallows

all have winged across the main'; but did he know that spiders also migrate and that in order to do so they make the 'gossamer' he talks about?

In the autumn the spider-population of some rough pasture may reach astronomical proportions, literally millions to the acre. When the weather is auspicious, the young spiders climb to the top of bush and fence, face the wind, raise their abdomens and produce strands of silk. These float off on the breeze, bearing the spiders with them for considerable distances, in what is sometimes called 'ballooning'. But sometimes, more spectacularly, as now, there is a 'rain of wool', when the earth becomes patchworked with silk. This, too, is made by the young spiders but is nothing to do with migration. Their action is triggered off by a sudden rise in temperature and the result has a fairyland charm especially when the gossamer's delicacy is enhanced by dew and sunlight.

This morning I really did stand and stare.

(ABOVE) Cattle, like horses, took a long time to reach their present form. Even our recent ancestors would look with wonder at modern animals. However, the eighteenth century also saw a vast improvement: between 1710 and 1795 the weight of both cattle and sheep sold at London's Smithfield Market more than doubled.

(LEFT) Evening sky in Devon. If you know your own patch of sky and possess a barometer, your predictions will be more reliable than any weather forecast.

✳

Laska, my labrador bitch, is in disgrace, if only temporarily. She came into the drawing-room stinking palpably of some fearful carrion she had joyfully rolled in. Fortunately, like all labradors, she adores swimming, so presently when we go down to the river, she will immediately plunge in and be rid of that repulsive reminder of her canine origins.

For the dog is by nature a scavenger and carrion-eater, as well as being a killer. To appreciate this you have only to watch the earnest lengths to which it will go in burying a bone, often in a seedbed, or simply and symbolically by scuffing the blanket in the dog basket over it. But unlike the squirrel which so often forgets the hazel-nuts it buries at random, the dog will always return to dig up its treasure, preferably when it is abominably high.

This scavenging aspect of the dog's origins is the subject of a theory put forward by Konrad Lorenz in *Man meets Dog,* and which seems to me perfectly tenable. He describes the dog's far-off progenitor, of the jackal type, howling mournfully round the confines of a primitive camp, its eyes green in the firelight; eager for a share of the meat it can smell. For a long time it is afraid of the crackling fire round which the skin-clad humans squat, but at length the dog-jackal plucks up courage and makes off with a discarded bone or lump of gristle.

The canine ancestor associates Man with food and takes to skulking after him when he goes off hunting with his companions. A deer breaks cover some distance away, too big for the 'dog' to tackle; the men have missed it, so the dog-jackal raises its supplicating voice to draw their attention to it. Gradually the primitive hunters take note, they realize the significance of the persistent and peculiar canine cry – and we have the start of the closest relationship Man has ever formed with another animal.

And that evening, as Laska puts her head on my knee and, out of her soulful brown eyes, begs forgiveness for her unsavoury habits, I wonder how many thousands of canine generations have passed since her distant ancestor scavenged round that camp-fire.

✳

'Yur,' cried Mr Maddowcroft, riding back from the moor where he had been having a look at his Galloways. I happened to be at the front gate and his pony Joey thrust a tangled head over the top bar to pass the time of day, while the farmer, a ruddy-cheeked, moorland centaur, gazed down on me with the inherent superiority of the horseman. 'I just see'd some'at would've interested you, zno!'

He had been riding along in the lee of a drystone wall to see if it was worth repairing, for he has one or two rough fields on the edge of the moor. (Drystone walling is, alas, a fading skill, and the gap will no doubt be stopped with wire netting and stakes.) Something moving not far away caught his eye and he saw that it was a fox.

'I bean't saying a word of a lie,' Mr Maddowcroft leaned down from the saddle in his eagerness, while Joey snorted explosively as if in corroboration. 'I could a'most a-sworn that ole fox was tipsy or leastaways had taken leave of ees senses. There 'er were, a-chasing of his tail like a mad thing. Going round and round and round like a whirligig. Then he flung himself on the ground – like Joey here sometimes has a roll – '

I listened intently, knowing more must be coming.

'Then,' puffed Mr Maddowcroft, quite breathless by now, 'I spied a couple of rabbits a-watching, too. Not twenty paces away, zno? And they rabbits, they stared like they was mussmerized – as if they had paid to get in. And all that while the cunning ole rascal of a fox was getting closer and closer to the silly creatures – '

'Go on,' I urged.

Mr Maddowcroft's face fell and he shook his head.

'I don't know what 'twas,' he said, tugging at the reins reproachfully. 'Maybe old Joey here snorted or the old fox got our scent. But all of a sudden, up he leaps and skedaddles one way and them two rabbits, they scoot t'other way – '

'Ah' I echoed Mr Maddowcroft's disappointment. I would indeed have liked to see the vulpine ploy, especially if it had reached the climax the fox had intended. I have heard and read about this trick of approaching rabbits under cover of an apparently zany but really very calculated performance; and of similar performances by stoats which have writhed and tumbled in crazy contortions with the object of drawing within striking distance of an audience of birds enthralled in curiosity.

October

Season of mists and mellow fruitfulness,
Close bosom-friend of the maturing sun –

Keats's is the conventional aspect of autumn, but for me the word always conjures up images of bonfires crackling away in field and garden, the blue smoke rising in eddying whorls bewilderingly complex and delicate: how on earth are those diaphanous veils formed?

Some people say you shouldn't burn anything, but it is impossible to compost all garden waste, such as the haulms of potato, bean and pea, not to mention docks and nettles, and anyway potash benefits the soil. The garden bonfire at the end of the season is always immensely satisfying – after all, you are starting the process of preparing the ground for next year. But the unfailing thrill and wonder of a good bonfire touches a deeper, infinitely older chord in our make-up. Fire, the use of it, the means of creating it, was Man's greatest single discovery.

At the outset when he encountered fire caused by one natural means or another, he must have been terrified and fled before it. But when, no doubt by chance, he discovered it was not necessarily a fearful ravaging creature consuming all before it and that it could be fed, maintained and controlled, it began fundamentally to change his entire existence. He could warm himself at it, he no longer needed to fear the prowling beasts or the cold – and indeed he may have used fire to expel certain beasts from their caves where he took refuge from the rigours of the Ice Age.

At first he had to carry the captive fire around with him, and there are still primitive people who, while making use of fire, do not possess the skill to create a new fire. *They* carry smouldering wood from place to place as they travel. One can perfectly understand the symbolism of certain 'eternal' flames that must never be allowed to go out. The man who discovered the means of producing fire by friction must indeed have seemed to be a magician.

But as well as protection from cold and wild beasts, fire drew people closer together: the fire, the hearth, became the focal point of their lives, and it is no exaggeration to say that literature sprang from the fireside, too. For it was round it that the first story-tellers told their tales, based perhaps on the day's hunting

Red deer stag with his hinds on a misty autumn morning in Bradgate Park, Leicestershire. In the wild it is usually only during the rutting season that red deer stags and hinds consort. At other times the hinds tend to keep to themselves, together with young calves of the previous year. The stags live singly or with a solitary younger attendant or in small groups.

and the weird creatures they had encountered. Fantasy came easily to them, for much of what they experienced they did not understand; so fiction was a natural process to them.

So, leaning upon a garden-fork, while a robin twitters nearby, my face tingling from the heat, I am sharing, at an infinite distance, and in a faint, atrophied way, the thrill and wonder that one of my far-off ancestors experienced in the mists of time. And when with the children we bake potatoes in the ashes, aren't we savouring a little of the surprised gratification of the man who first discovered that cooked food was more enjoyable than raw? What if his food did fall in the fire accidentally, the result was the same.

How great a matter a little fire kindleth!

✳

In his various moorland haunts, it is now a time of agony for the red deer stag. He tries to cool his fever by rolling in his favourite mud-wallow until his flanks are plastered with slime and he is altogether a horrendous sight. He bends his muscular neck and rends the earth with his antlers in a frenzy of rage, scattering gobbets of soil and moss.

And he thrusts out his fantastic branchy head and roars — they call it belling, though it has no resemblance to the wildest bell ringing out to the wild sky: the word comes from the same stem as bellow. In fact, the sound is like a cross between the grunting cough of a lion and the moaning of a bull. This mournful plaint echoes through the combes — and is heard by other stags who take up the challenge. At times you can hear a dozen stags challenging and counter-challenging, the effect confused by the fact that the animals are constantly on the move.

The most anxious among the stags is the leader of the hinds. The danger to the integrity of his harem comes not only or chiefly from his immediate challenger, but from the hangers-on skulking at the edge of the scene. These stags wait until the two main contenders are confronting each other, and then attempt to sneak in, hoping to split up the herd and drive off some of the hinds. Because the more splendid of the stags are pre-occupied, distracted by hatred of each other, it means that very often the hinds are served by inferior animals. The survival of the fittest does not always apply.

Although several stags may be challenging at the same time, the leader of the herd knows there is really only one other stag who matters, at least for the time being. In a scene of urgent bedlam the two rivals trot closer, awe-inspiring in their animal strength and fury, neck and shoulders bristling with a mantle of coarse hair. One almost expects to see fire and smoke issue from their nostrils instead of their vaporous breath.

Each stag advances again, pauses, groans hollowly, then rushes upon the other. With a furious clattering of antlers they meet and stagger with the shock. Recovering, they fence and strike again with such force one would think to see them stunned or their antlers splintered.

With legs splayed out to keep their balance, they strike again and again, pushing, feinting, their proud necks bowed. They stand hoof to hoof, as it were, and fight it out with grunting intensity, all else forgotten. Time after time there is a violent clattering as each stag tries to pierce his rival with his brow tine — the short tines nearest the head that are the real weapons of the red deer. Their antlers bleed, their dishevelled sides heave, savage noises rise from their swollen throats.

But it does not last long. It *has* been known for the antlers to be locked together when both of the contestants eventually perish, but that is extremely rare. Very soon one or other of the stags knows he is beaten and withdraws, roaring defiance, to avoid further injury. It is highly unusual for wild animals to 'fight to the death'; their motto is rather live to fight another day. The exceptions are perhaps the mole and the shrew, bearing out the adage that the smaller they are the fiercer they come. They can be particularly beastly to each other at mating-time.

As far as the red deer are concerned, it is not only the vanquished who is willing to break off the encounter: the victor

(ABOVE) Stubble burning in autumn makes the land look like a battle zone through which a ravaging army has passed.

(ABOVE, RIGHT) Swallows gathering together prior to migration. Two hundred years ago men were not at all certain that birds migrated.

Linnaeus believed that swallows hibernated and Gilbert White was only convinced about migration by evidence from his brother who was

chaplain to the Gibraltar garrison and saw large numbers of birds passing over the island at different seasons of the year.

now has the pressing task of re-establishing control of the hinds, whose needs are just as earnest as his and they don't mind who fulfils them.

*

On the grassland, cropped close already by cattle and sheep, and now beginning to be cropped still closer by the first frosts, fieldfares and redwings, constant companions, advance in serried ranks that become more numerous as you watch. They are handsome birds, the fieldfares or 'blue-backs' as they are sometimes called, with erect carriage like that of their cousin the missel-thrush, with subtle greys and browns and buffs and blacks that become more impressive the more closely you study them. The kingfisher is a flaming feathered barb of colour, the bullfinch is testimony to a divine palette, but these thrushes (and all their family) are painted in subdued tones not evident to a cursory glance.

The fieldfares seem to be always playing a game of grandmother's steps – pattering a few paces then halting alertly to watch and listen. In contrast, the redwings are dumpier birds, but they too are fine-looking, especially with their warm reddish brown eponymous patch under the wings and along the flanks. They are less robust birds than the fieldfares whose aggressive churring more aptly sums up their character. The blue-backs cry *chak chak chak* as they settle in the hawthorns to feast on the bright red peggles, but when they fly they chuckle and whistle, perhaps in appreciation of being well-fed. The quieter redwings say *chup chup chup* softly – and you can, incidentally, sometimes hear them as they pass overhead at night, especially when they are first coming in from the far north.

We think of bird-migrants mainly in terms of warblers and swallows and cuckoos, bringing with them a breath of the many-hued south that will, we hope, tinge our own summer with a little warmth. But when the winter-migrants arrive we are already more shut in, literally and metaphorically, and fear the weather their arrival presages. Yet nothing can be more thrilling than the clangour of wild geese winging exultantly overhead on their journey from the dark, brooding north, or more moving than the thought of the little-finger-size goldcrest (which used to be known as the 'Woodcock-pilot' because it heralded the coming of that other winter visitor) facing the perils of the North Sea to seek shelter in some English conifer-stand. And again, what more handsome than the stark blacks and whites and greys of the great grey shrike, that pugnacious bird with the hooked beak, or the rarely seen waxwing, with its prominent crest and red and yellow markings?

But summer or winter, bird-migration is one of the most wonderful and mysterious aspects of nature. A great many theories have been put forward to explain how birds can navigate often vast distances. How, for instance, does the young cuckoo, which never knows its parents, find its way unaided to Africa? How do certain young waders migrate from Arctic regions on their own *after* their parents have flown?

Of course there is much 'hereditary' knowledge that helps, while in addition birds must get to know, collectively or individually, such topographical features as rivers, coastlines, valleys and the like. But the case of the young cuckoos and waders shows that birds must possess some sort of in-built navigation apparatus. Not only is there the self-evidence of these natural migrations, but various field-tests have shown an astonishing homing instinct in birds. Noddy and sooty terns, for example, taken from their nesting-grounds round the Gulf of Mexico, have found their way back over hundreds of miles of unknown territory without hesitation.

The biggest factor or mechanism in this do-it-yourself navigation kit seems to be an innate sense of time, a sort of internal clock, which enables birds to take into consideration the time of day and an ability to make allowance for the position of sun or stars overhead, just as a human navigator does with his instruments. In this connection experiments have been carried out by placing birds in a planetarium and recording their reactions when the stars have been blacked-out or re-oriented. We are still attempting to find a completely satisfactory explanation of the

marvels of bird-migration, though this time-light theory is the most feasible.

Earthbound Man has taken to the air perilously with the aid of ingenious but not infallible machines, but nothing can match the fragile skill and strength of these feathered wings that reach their most wonderful expression in their transworld journeys.

✻

We should have been alerted straightaway; on the bird-table just outside the kitchen a mouse was busy foraging. The normal pensioners were quite unnerved by this intrusion. The tits and chaffinches even raised their hackles in a manner of speaking. Only those bullies of the bird-table, the truculent nuthatches, threatened with their long beaks, crouching ready for action.

The mouse was far too absorbed to heed even them, especially when he came across a small knot-hole in the table (I measured it afterwards and found it to be less than the circumference of a 1p piece). Perhaps he was a connoisseur of holes in general or maybe some crumb had become lodged in this one. Anyway, he became positively frenzied in his attempts to get through – or *into*, as he probably thought – that particular hole.

Repeatedly he dived at it, thrusting in his forequarters, while his sleek haunches and tail wriggled in an ecstasy of eagerness and frustration. At times it seemed as if he was stuck, but each time he backed out again, though with some difficulty. He took a turn or two round the bird-table and appeared to be giving up the attempt. But he was made of sterner stuff and resumed his frantic efforts. Eventually he absolutely forced himself through the hole – and got through to the underside, from which he descended by way of the post. He paused a long time at the bottom, looking like a mouse that had emerged far too rapidly from a decompression chamber. Or perhaps he was cogitating over why that hole had turned out not to be a real hole.

Not long afterwards our amusement was rudely dispelled when a small side drawer in an oak-press in the spare bedroom was opened. The Roger & Gallet soap that had been stored in it had been pared down to half its original size; the drawer was littered with signs of a prolonged murine occupation.

Evidently those mice had grown surfeited by a diet of soap, even expensive stuff. They had gone downstairs and next put in a brief appearance in the drawing-room, where, after finding tell-tale marks on the top of an armchair, I surprised one of the mice sitting on the record-player. It took refuge on a curtain which it climbed without the slightest difficulty. Nor did it have any difficulty in taking evasive action.

But the favoured snuggery of the mice was in the kitchen and some of them seemed to have been cut off from HQ: that night members of the squad almost ate down the communicating doors in their efforts to break through. Little heaps of paint and wood shavings lay at the foot of each door in succession. The next night we made a point of leaving the doors open so as not to discommode these four-footed sappers – or suffer any more damage, especially as the doors were newly painted.

There was now nothing for it but traps. The setting of them coincided with my having to be away for a few days. My wife was horrified one morning to find one of the traps sprung, but no sign of a victim. She was even more horrified a day or two later by olfactory evidence that a mouse had been mortally wounded but had managed to take itself off to die.

For two whole years we had been begging our local builder to come and do various small jobs that needed attention. Yes, he would come, he would come, he would come – but he never came. Yet when my wife sent this SOS about the dead mouse he was an the doorstep within half an hour. He took up the floorboards and located the offending corpse; a nice instance of right priorities. Those odd jobs still haven't been done.

But one trapped mouse did not solve our problems. On my return, my wife had yet another horror story. They had been singing, or at least one of the mice had been singing. She had been busy sewing one evening; everything was utterly still – and suddenly she had heard this peculiar little singing. She looked at me askance, expecting me to question her sanity. That mouse was positively singing, she persisted.

Gratefully, I suggested – after all, they have a lot to be thankful for, board and lodging, warmth – or of course it might have been singing a requiem for its defunct companion. That we were not amused was quite plain. I tell you it was singing! Well, old Edward Topsell spoke of a 'whiner' among mice – and Walter de la Mare once mentioned a mouse that sings in a way 'quite distinct from the common squeaking, shrilling and shriek-ing. It resembles the slow trill of a distant and sleepy canary, but sweeter and more domestic, and is as pleasant a thing to hear behind a wainscot, as it is to watch the creatures gambolling. Whatever mischief their ravagings may cause, may I never live under a roof wherein (Cat or no Cat) there isn't an inch of house-room (and an occasional crumb of cheese) for Mistress Mouse!'

But I was sorry to disabuse both my wife and, posthumously, Walter de la Mare. That pretty mousy singing is caused not by any small contentment: it is due to inflammation of the lungs, which some mice suffer from. In other words they have a bronchial condition.

There is only one answer to our problem and that is to borrow a cat from Mr Maddowcroft, whose place swarms with felines. I don't know how our Laska will take it, but she's no good: deadly with rats, she somehow feels that mice are in a different category. Once, when I was sawing wood in the shippon, she was stretched out in the sun. A mouse emerged from some crevice close by. Dog and mouse simply and literally

Young house mice. In his *Historie of Four-footed Beastes*, Edward Topsell catalogued mice as short, small, fearful, peaceable, rustik, ridiculous, or country mice, the urban or city mouse, the greedy, wary, unhappy, harmful, black, obscene, little whiner, biter and earthly mouse. Some people, he said, believed that white mice fed on snow.

touched noses, after which Laska went back to sleep and the mouse trickled away under the wall.

Only a cat will reassure my wife while these small lodgers are in residence.

> *There was a wee bit mousikie,*
> *That lived in Gilberaty, O,*
> *It couldna get a bite o' cheese,*
> *For cheetie-poussie-cattie, O.*

> *It said unto the cheesikie,*
> *'Oh fain wad I be at ye, O,*
> *If't were na for the cruel paws*
> *O' cheetie-poussie-cattie, O'.*

PS or Stop Press! No cat at any price! I have just caught one of Mr Maddowcroft's marmalade monsters in *flagrante delicto* slaying a robin on the bird-table. There is nothing for it but to put up with our small visitors and hope to be entertained by their tiny singing!

✳

Every couple of weeks or so the inimitable sound of metal clanging on metal rings out from the riding-stables at the corner of the lane. Clink, clink, clink, it is a simple song that always thrills me although I am no horseman, for it has echoed through the centuries. The travelling smith is paying his regular visit, all his gear, anvil, hammers, tongs, bellows, portable brazier, stock of iron, loaded into his little Ford van which sinks on its springs with the burden.

For some years it seemed as if the blacksmith was a vanished species. Gone before him, except for a few relics, and discounting the race-course, was the horse. Under the spreading chestnut tree the village smithy stood silent, the bellows no longer breathed the embers into a roaring bed of heat, the sparks no longer fled gleefully up through the great canopy over the forge. No longer could one experience the strange, exciting, daunting atmosphere of the smithy, with its alternating flame and murk, the acrid, nose-prickling smell of red-hot iron plunged in water, the tang of burning hoof and singed hair as a shoe was being fitted. The smith's sons or grandsons had gone off to jobs in the cities, perhaps to some iron-foundry, or in some cases had started up the local garage, crawling under oily motor-cars in a 'diagnostic bay' instead of putting a sturdy work-horse's feet in trim for the ploughing-season.

But then, gradually, leisure-time expanded, people became more mobile and could get out into the countryside in a matter of minutes, while simultaneously Mr Thelwell invented horse-riding as a pastime for the masses, especially masses of small, severe-

looking girls, though many adults joined in, too, and in the course of time the small girls became adult and continued their devotions to *Equus caballus caballus*. Riding as a fashionable pastime was no longer confined to the privileged few.

The equine population increased tenfold – and a horse needs to be re-shod every five or six weeks or so. This was the cue for the re-entry of the blacksmith – the farrier, if you wish to be exact: his work is confined to horses, the blacksmith does other iron-work as well. All farriers are blacksmiths, but not all blacksmiths are farriers. Anyway, it is mainly as a travelling smith that he is now seen, but in spite of all inventions –

Pink-footed geese *(Anser brachyrhychus)*. Seventy years ago Gilfrid Hartley wrote, of wild geese in general: 'There is a romance about this great bird which is wanting in all the others; he comes from so far; his home is so mysterious and unknown.'

A smith at work. Although Longfellow's fustian words about the mighty smith with large and sinewy hands working at the village smithy under the spreading chestnut tree have often been parodied the smith played a key part in Man's history.

supersonic travel, computers – he is still surrounded by an aura of wonder and awe, even though he is like some high priest who has been forced to quit his real tabernacle and perform his rites in the open air.

The smith was really in at the beginning, it might be said. Flint, bronze, all counted in Man's onward march, but it was, always acknowledging his fundamental mastery of fire, the discovery of how to smelt iron that was one of his most significant advances; the realization that out of certain kinds of soil or slag he could forge all manner of tools and weapons was, relatively, more important than all the inventions that followed. How thrilling it would be to know in detail how this startling discovery came about, to see the first haphazard step, the pondering over its significance, followed by the tentative, elementary process of making iron.

The smith was more than just a mighty man, he was an awesome figure, a magician, a jealous craftsman who kept his secrets to himself and his immediate kin. For me, Kipling's story, *The Knife and the Naked Chalk,* has always vividly symbolized the turning-point of iron in man's life.

The pastoral people of the downs were sorely pressed by the wolf – Grey Shepherd, Feet-in-the-Night – which ravaged their

(ABOVE) These apple-pickers in a Kent orchard were photographed in the 1950s, but orchards like this one do still exist despite the advent of that fruitarian equivalent of sliced bread, the Golden Delicious apple.

(LEFT) Processing cider in Worcestershire in 1938. At that time cider was looked upon as a countryman's drink, but during the past decade or two it has become increasingly popular with urban Man. Robert Browning, however, clearly didn't like it:

I heard a sound as of scraping
tripe,
And putting apples wondrous ripe,
Into a cider-press's gripe.

flocks. It had little fear of brittle arrows and blunt spears made of flint that flaked treacherously. They were in despair, there seemed no answer to the savagery of the Beast. But then the Flint-worker, their chieftain, learned of the Children of the Night who possessed the secret of the Magic Knife – in other words, the secret of iron-making.

At great peril, for it meant venturing into the dread forests, he journeyed into their hidden country. Offering them meat and milk and wool, he begged them to share their secret. But to make

Cutcombe Cattle Auction, Weddon Cross, Somerset. The cattle have been penned and are being numbered prior to being sold. Nowadays, because of improved methods of transport, far fewer markets exist. In the days when cattle had to travel on the hoof and men had to travel on foot or on horseback every small town had its own market.

certain of his good faith and earnestness, they demanded more than that: they demanded the sacrifice of his right eye.

So desperate were the needs of his people he unflinchingly agreed to this, in return for which the Children of the Night showed him 'how they melted their red stone and made the Magic Knives of it. They told me the charms they sang over the fires and at the beatings.'

The Flint-worker's people were saved. Everywhere the Beast ran away from this fearsome new weapon with which the people were now armed. Now men no longer trembled in fear as they tended their flocks.

Round the young smith in the stableyard stand a gaggle of school-children who have come out to ride. As they watch him work, fascinated as one always is by someone else's skill, I wonder if he or they realize what a long link in human history he represents. In my childhood the blacksmith was a thrilling, dark, saturnine, almost unearthly figure, terrifying in his ability, with the aid of searing fire, to hammer and shape and bend iron into submission as if it was mere dough and then, equally astonishingly, to cradle the hoof of some seventeen-hand equine monster in his leather-covered lap while he fitted its shoe.

✻

To market, to market, to buy a fat pig,
Home again, home again, jiggity-jig.
To market, to market, a gallop, a trot,
To buy some meat to put in the pot.

The leisurely days implied by such folk-rhymes have long since disappeared. Or have they? I sometimes go to market with Mr Maddowcroft – just for an outing. It does not happen very often, though *he* goes every week almost religiously, indeed far more regularly than to church. Whenever I do go with him, I look around at all the strident chaos of backing lorries, vociferous drivers, gigantic two-tiered cattle-trucks, and the serried ranks of motor-cars barricading the church-square, and I realize that for all the superficial changes, market-day remains much the same.

True, instead of driving into 'town' in his smart, varnished trap drawn by a mettlesome pony whose hooves clip-clop importantly on the cobbles of some hostelry's courtyard, the farmer arrives in state in a solid Vauxhall or the ubiquitous Land Rover (to which, surely, the agricultural industry should raise a monument). He is better dressed, too, being more prosperous than his pre-war counterpart, regulation tweed cap, tweed jacket, sometimes cord breeches, though wellingtons have replaced those impressive leather gaiters that used to shine so brilliantly a dog could see its reflection in them.

But behind the wheel of those opulent looking motor-cars, when you can discern them under the mud, and inside those chunky clothes, people remain much the same as they ever were. Especially here at market, which transforms them. Everyone becomes larger than life: though many folk are pretty sizeable already, such as those plump and jolly old countrywomen who preside over their stalls in the pannier market selling rich brown eggs (real eggs) or vegetables that look as if they had been touched up with furniture polish.

People talk more loudly than usual. In fact, they shout, their eyes sparkling and rolling as if they were afraid of missing something, their teeth flashing in cavernous mouths. Well, of course you have to shout because of the din: the bleating of sheep, the bellowing of cows, the racket of vehicles, the cursing of white-coated attendants, and presently, when business starts the verbal acrobatics of the auctioneer. But people also shout for sheer joy. It's as if they are drinking down great draughts of life and are eager to consume as much of it as possible before returning to the humdrum tasks on their farms and anxiety about the size of the next milk-cheque and the bill for fertilizers.

For that is half the point of going to market, as Mr Maddowcroft admits. You may not have so much as a brace of geese to sell, you may not need so much as a bundle of clothes-pegs sold by some hawker. But the sale-fever takes hold of you willy-nilly and you hang over the iron railings critically surveying the naked pigs and the thick-woolled sheep lying in fresh straw yellower than a Norseman's hair, or you even test the udder of some sleek cow or twist the tail of a knock-kneed calf to make it stand up.

But buying and selling are only part of going to market. You go for the pleasure of meeting people, having a good old gossip, chewing over that vaster Common Market, lamb exports, Green Pounds and all, perhaps as you sit in one of the pubs eating steak and kidney with an abominable pre-fabricated triangle of pastry instead of real old-fashioned suet pudding rich in gravy, although it'll more likely be so-called bar-food or even hot dogs at a travelling snack-bar.

Market-day is still an essential part of English country life; indeed, markets are human history to a great extent. Their establishment marked another of those turning-points, after settled farming had started to produce a modest surplus and also as needs grew. People with goods or produce to sell began to bring these to some convenient place, at the crossing of a river or the meeting of various tracks where they would be most likely to encounter other folk with whom they could trade.

The 'farmers' brought their livestock, other men brought salt for the preservation of meat. The smiths would come with their iron ware, the stone-cutters with querns for grinding corn, the tar-burners would bring their ointments for use against animal ailments. And so the first towns began to be established on the spots where those early Mr Maddowcrofts used to foregather!

November

I went over to Mr Maddowcroft to cadge some plastic sacks, the kind that so frequently litter farmland nowadays: I intended putting them down on a path difficult to keep free of weeds and cover them with stone chippings. I have done it before and it is highly effective.

When I got there Mr Maddowcroft was walking across the farmyard followed by a veritable herd of cats. Tails up and quivering, they jostled about his ankles, followed in his wake, raced ahead, pirouetted round, leapt over each other. I counted no fewer than seventeen of them, of all ages and sizes and colours – 'some white, some rede, some blacke, some skewed and speckled in the face and in the eares.'

I could certainly have had my choice had I wished. But well aware that it wasn't the Sparrow with his little arrow who had killed my particular Cock Robin, I am very emphatically anti-cat.

'And that's not all of them, by hundreds,' said Mr Maddowcroft with a touch of pride as he halted at the black-tarred barn-door while the cats, all females by the look of them, scrimmaged agilely round the splashes of milk falling from the tin jug he was carrying. 'There's a whole heap more roundabout. They're regular travelling cats, some of 'em. They come and go as the vancy takes them. I saw one a mile away the other morning across the main road. That one there's been gone fourteen days till now. They go over to your place, too.'

'I know,' I reply, acidly. 'They get on to the bird-table and –'

'They never come into the house, though,' Mr Maddowcroft went on, dismissively if not apropos. 'There's not a mouse in the place. No more a rat.'

I remained silent. The subject was painful.

He opened the creaking door and had to steady himself after a feline charge had threatened to trip him up. But there was no squabbling, no yowling, just polite eagerness. They knew their ration was forthcoming; farm cats never lack sustenance where cows are kept.

Even when cursing them for bird-killing or scratching up your seedbeds, you cannot suppress a certain admiration for cats, their lissome bonelessness, daintiness, independence and condescending and often opportunistic affection. 'It is needless,' wrote Edward Topsell in his Elizabethan *Historie of Four-footed Beastes,* 'to spend any time about the cat's loving nature to man,

Few Teddy Bears have been pressed into service as scarecrows, but this Lancashire one provides the headpiece for an imposing figure. The dead crow in the scarecrow's left hand failed to have the desired deterrent effect on the neighbourhood birds. Perhaps that's why the scarecrow wears a somewhat dismayed expression?

how she flattereth by rubbing her skinne against one's legges, how she whurleth with her voyce to beg and complain, another to testifie her delight and pleasure, another among her own kind by flattring, by hissing, by spitting, insomuch as some have thought that they have a peculiar intelligible language among themselves.'

But perhaps respect rather than admiration is one of the most ancient reactions to the cat. The Egyptians venerated cats and painted them in company with their Pharaohs; they wondered at the cat's astonishing eyes and fancied that these waxed and waned in accordance with the phases of the moon. They deified cats and embalmed them with reverent care when they died.

In England during the Middle Ages cats were considered so valuable that a cat-tariff was established by law. Even before it opened its eyes a kitten was valued at one penny; tuppence was

In future this farm cat will wait in vain for opening time. Churns like these are rapidly becoming period pieces as dairy farmers are obliged to install bulks tanks in which to store their milk.

the price of an older kitten, while a cat that had already caught its first mouse was worth as much as fourpence, a considerable sum in those days. Heavy penalties were imposed on anyone who killed a cat from the Royal granaries. Attitudes that Mr Maddowcroft would undoubtedly have approved.

✻

Walking over the brow of a field of winter-wheat alongside which a footpath runs, I was startled to see a fantastic warrior rise up seemingly out of the earth as if in ambush. His apparent movement was an optical illusion caused by the rising ground and my own faraway thoughts: but the figure was there all right, a scarecrow in the shape of a Roman legionary complete with helmet and breast-plate, the product of someone's imagination

and derelict theatrical props acquired at a market-stall. Staring bleakly out of a cardboard face, as if offended by the task he had been put to, he stood there drunkenly, brandishing a cardboard short sword that was nailed to the broom-handle cross-piece — and as I passed closer it was evident that his martial-looking helmet was disrespectfully spattered with the whitewash of the rooks whose gleaming black mantles had contrasted so nicely with the vivid green daggers of wheat.

You do not encounter so many scarecrows or 'tattie-bogles' nowadays, but years ago they used to be a feature of the countryside, decked out in bowler hats and with pipes stuck in their mouths, like tramps who were earning a few pence for the next doss-house. Half a century or more ago, live scarecrows used to be employed, in the shape of wretched small boys armed with rattles or wooden clappers or tins full of pebbles or pails which they banged with sticks. This was variously known as bird-tending or crow-starving or crow-keeping. George Ewart Evans, in his *Where Beards Wag All*, quotes from a nineteenth-century Government report on this widespread practice — and the effect it had on children:

> *I found in the school (in question) an example of the physical ill results that sometimes are produced by early employment. Asking a question of a little boy I could not*

These farmyard cats wait expectantly for their share of the milk from the Jersey cow that can just be seen in the background. In return for keeping the mouse and rat population under control farm cats receive a daily reward of milk.

A salmon leaping upriver on the River Lledr at Betws-y-coed, Gwynedd. Two principal strains of salmon exist, the Atlantic species and a number of Pacific varieties. The Atlantic salmon is the finer, its flesh being greatly superior. It sometimes reaches the sea again after spawning; the Pacific varieties never do and the banks of the rivers in which they spawn are often littered with the bodies of spent fish.

These beech trees were photographed in Dorset in November. They have lost most of their leaves and the full beauty of their silvery barks is revealed.

hear his answer; when enquiring I was informed that the boy had been sent 'to keep birds' when he was only six years old, and lost his voice by shouting at them. He is now nine years of age and it is considered questionable if he will ever recover it.

Nowadays in fruit orchards at crucial times students can 'earn' useful money for the job of bird-minding.

*

Late one afternoon I was walking through a wood a few miles from here when, from some thirty or forty yards ahead there came the sound of something splashing violently in the little stream, scarcely more than a ditch, that flowed through deep, steep-sided banks. Mystified, I crept on cautiously, eager to know what could be making such an uninhibited noise. Surely it couldn't be an otter playing? A mallard having a bath? And yet it must be a fair-sized creature that was besporting itself.

At length I stealthily reached a point directly above the focal point of this aquatic pandemonium: four or five feet below me, oblivious to all else but their vital object, a pair of salmon were spawning. Dusky in the overhung stream but clearly visible, for the water was so shallow their backs were not even covered, the fish worked their way spasmodically upstream. The female regularly lashed her shoulders powerfully to and fro to make the 'redds' or troughs in the sandy bottom for her eggs, whereupon the male dashed in with furious urgency to fertilize them with his milt.

This continued for many yards until, eventually, because of fading light and bramble-brakes, I lost contact with them. In any case the splashing ceased. The salmon's work was done; posterity had been safeguarded. Afterwards, exhausted by the spawning, those two salmon would lose their graceful silvery, streamlined look. Their skin spongy, their flesh watery and inferior, their jaws hooked and ugly, they would float haplessly downriver as kelt, vastly different from the magnificent fish which as grilse had thrust upriver so athletically a few weeks ago, bars of iridescent silver in the spray of waterfall or weir, leaping, time after time if necessary, higher and higher, ten or eleven feet, obeying the irresistible urge to return to their native headwaters and perpetuate their race. Not for nothing did the Romans call the Salmon 'Salar', the Leaper.

One of the most splendid of fish, the most esteemed, the most expensive, both to catch and to eat, the salmon is also one of the most persecuted. As soon as the eggs are laid, the persecution starts. A female salmon produces nearly one thousand eggs for every pound of her weight: which means twenty thousand for even a modest sized fish such as I had been watching. Not all are even fertilized, many being washed away. Of those fertilized, eels

Throughout the country at least ten times as many salmon are caught by seine-net fishermen and others as by rod fishermen. Fresh-run salmon can usually be recognized by the sea-lice that remain on their bodies for four or five days after they enter the river.

devour large numbers; even dipper and water-shrew feed on them.

The incubation period of the surviving eggs varies with temperature conditions from five to twenty-one weeks. The fry that hatch out are known as alevins and, subsisting on the yolk-sac attached to their abdomen, they shelter as best they can among the stones of stream or riverbed for a couple of months, by which time they are little fish an inch in length. As befits what will be, if it survives, a spectacular fish going up to sixty or eighty pounds, the salmon's growth is slow. By the end of its first year it will be three or four inches in length; at two years, nearly six inches. It is now a salmon parr, its body marked with dark, oval-shaped bands, a red spot between each pair of these.

The persecution increases: pike, chub, trout, cannibalistic salmon, all plunder the infant fish; herons stalk the water on the look-out; kingfishers dive unerringly and beat their prey to death on a stone; mink are a growing hazard. But the once-maligned and now rare otter is more friend than foe to the salmon, for it catches large numbers of eels, which are perhaps the worst enemies of the salmon in its early stages.

The length of time the parr remains in this stage varies and is always longer in Arctic rivers. Usually, however, when it is two or three years old and anything between three and seven inches long, the distinctive parr bands and red spots disappear and the young fish takes on a handsome silvery appearance. It is now a smolt and it heads for the open sea, where it is beset by new enemies, including Man. Until recent times the movements of salmon once they took to the sea were a mystery. But then, nearly twenty years ago, Danish fishermen located their main feeding-grounds off Greenland. Before some sort of international control was effected, their avaricious netting brought salmon stocks in Canada and Britain to near-disaster and indeed the salmon is still in danger.

After a year or more, the smolt feels impelled to return to its native river, and its unerring ability to do so lies in its sense of smell (which is highly developed in fish). Just as ewe and lamb can recognize one another out of hundreds of sheep by their individual scent, so does the salmon know its own river, its own mother-river it could be said.

It is now a grilse in the peak of condition after the rich feeding

in the sea. In estuary and river the salmon run the gauntlet on every side. The seine-net fishermen encircle them, the rod-fishermen look to their 'flics made of the Hair of Bears, Hogs, Squirrels' tails, Camels, Dogs, Foxes, Badgers, Otters, Cows, abortive Calves and Colts, Outlandish Caddows' or whatever they use nowadays. And poachers go about their nefarious business.

Once upon a time the poacher used to be a kind of folk-hero. But in modern times, with salmon fetching £5 a pound and smoked salmon twice as much, he is a highly organized unscrupulous thug, with explosives, poison, fast cars, collapsible boats, even snorkels, and monofilament nets which are almost invisible even in clear water in daylight.

But of course one of the worst enemies of the salmon is pollution. In bygone years they used regularly to ascend rivers such as the Seine, the Rhine and the Thames – witness the old tales of apprentices complaining about too much salmon on their menu. Maybe one day salmon will return to William Morris's 'clear Thames bordered by its gardens green' for progress has been made in cleansing the river.

Some of the grilse ascend the rivers in autumn, immediately on returning from the sea; others hang about until the spring. But

(*LEFT*) The earth is generous, but the soil must be coaxed and prepared. Here the stubble is being disc-harrowed to remove the surface trash before ploughing begins. Obviously this procedure finds favour with the starlings.

(*ABOVE*) Geese were domesticated as early as Neolithic times, long before other kinds of poultry. The goose recommended itself to Man by its readiness to eat far more than necessary, which not only made it ideal for fattening but also rendered it too heavy to fly.

once they do start their upriver journey they thrust on with muscular resolution (and a salmon can swim at twenty miles an hour or more) to fulfil the life-cycle of their race. Would my salmon be among the few to get back to the nourishing sea, regain their powers and return to the woodland ditch to breed again? Probably not; the odds are stacked against them.

*

Is it imagination, or do the geese begin to cock an anxious eye at me — or is it the reflection of my own qualms at the prospect of their demise?

Gaggling excitedly, they come flying towards me as I go out with their feed. They are only just able to become airborne and labour across the field two or three feet above the ground. Then with a mighty thrashing they land and run forward with wings still half raised, as if to protect their food in the manner of hawks. Their cries grow muffled and then subside, for their heads are in the trough almost before the mash has been tipped into it.

Before long they will have to be shut up to fatten off and I shall feel horribly guilty. 'Who is going to kill them?' a friend demanded accusingly when he heard of my keeping geese. (He sat at table enjoying a succulent lamb chop.) 'Somebody has got to do the job,' I answered defensively.

All the same, I am uneasy, and shall feel a traitor when the crucial moment comes. I shall miss their warning gaggle as someone comes along the lane, for they are formidable watch-dogs, as the Gauls once found to their cost. I shall miss their arrogant ways, their fierce hissing and snaking necks as the unfortunate postman encounters them. I shall miss seeing them parade in line astern across the field to drive the little pigs away from *their* food and then come marching back when they have had their stolen fill.

Now they waddle away from their hopper, conversing in satisfied tones. Suddenly they cock their heads skyward and set up an agitated gaggling and honking. Are there wild geese passing high overhead, far out of sight, that have upset them? They flap their wings, longingly, it seems, but they cannot become airborne again, for they have eaten too well.

I regard them appraisingly. They are fine birds, a gander and three geese. Would it not be more prudent to keep them for breeding purposes next spring. . .

*

'Look at thiccy hedges,' snorts old Arthur contemptuously, as we drive back from the market-town where we had happened to pick him up. 'They just comes along with a master great machine and slash slash slash and the result's a crying shame to man and nature, zno. Bean't no pride in that, midear.'

And he puffs more furiously than ever at his nubbly little pipe, as if to exorcize the offending sight.

Well might he criticize, for the hedges we were passing looked mauled and mutilated, a mass of stark white wounds and jagged ends, though maybe they will bush out next growing season. But the old man knew what he was talking about, for he was a true representative of a vanishing skill, that of the hedger. Seventy-five at least, he still works here and there, 'in and out', as he puts it, for anyone who prefers real handiwork, however slow by comparison, to the crude efforts of a young man on a machine.

A gnomelike figure, seemingly impervious to the weather except to acquire an ever deeper nutbrown hue, Arthur limps around clad mainly in real hessian sacks – one of them unstitched along the bottom seam so as to form a hood – which he treasures as if they were his Sunday best. Layering, laying and cutting, pleaching, it depends on the particular region what it is called, but the skill is the same. Pleaching is especially a Midland and Cotswold term, I believe – meaning simply to twine, interlace, tangle. It is a word Shakespeare uses several times, as in *Henry V*:

> Her hedges even-pleached
> Like prisoners wildly overgrown with hair
> Put forth disorder'd twigs.

The art of hedging has almost disappeared. H. J. Massingham wrote: 'To the hedger with his axe, his billhook, his maul (a clublike mallet for driving in stakes), and his horsehide mittens, England owes the preservation of what hedges are left to her.'

185

NOVEMBER

What is a hedge? In some parts of the country drystone walls are referred to as 'hedges'. The art of drystone walling requires as much skill as hedging and, like the hedger, the builder of drystone walls is a vanishing species.

With his billhook, his principal tool, Arthur slices part way through the branches of hawthorn and hazel and elder just far enough for them to be bent over almost horizontally, interwoven with each other and some on either side of the saplings which he leaves wherever possible, though in addition he rams in upright stakes where necessary with the butt end of his axe. He knows to a nicety how far to slice through the layered branches, for he must avoid going in so far that he cuts off the flow of sap and prevents their continued growth. And he always makes an undercut, thus leaving the branch less exposed to the weather. The saplings he leaves standing are essential not only for the construction or maintenance of a hedge, but because they will in theory grow into the hedgerow trees that are or should be such a feature of the countryside and are so valuable as shade for livestock.

'I see some pictures on the telly, t'other night,' says Arthur, almost invisible behind indignant smoke. 'Up country, eastaways – ah, East Angly, that was it. And they'd a' chopped down all the hedges, bull-dozied all the banks. My soul, it looked like that girt desert-land where Arabs lives, and the dust was blowing some'at cruel. Ah, I woulden like to live in country like that, zno. 'Twoulden be proper, without thiccy hedges.'

Arthur was perhaps not quite right there. For typical though the hedgerow is, it has not always been such a feature of the English countryside. It was only when the uneconomic 'open field' system began to be abandoned in Tudor times that the hedge really came into its own, though needless to say it had existed to some extent before. But now it has made up for lost time! Of all the many charms even of our contracting land, the hedgerow must rank high. Bedecked with wild roses, embraced by bush vetch and convolvulus, flanked by hogweed, hemlock and hound's tongue, baited with deadly nightshade, fragrant with honeysuckle, rich with blackberry, bullace, rowan and crab-apple, flashing with the wings of all the countless birds that make their homes in it, teeming with a tiny jungle-life of all the insects and their small assailants, passing cover for fox and stoat, a good hedgerow is as rewarding a beat for a nature-lover as many a tract ten times its size.

Yet what exactly is a hedge? Arthur would be in no doubt (though often he has to exercise an additional skill, that of 'steeping' when he is obliged to repair the bank on which a hedge sometimes stands). But when I was down in Cornwall recently a farmer-friend referred to his drystone wall as a hedge – and drystone-walling is an art in itself. What is more, not far from where he lives, there runs between Lerryn and Looe the so-called Giant's Hedge, or the vestiges of it, and that is an ancient earthwork built originally for defensive purposes. In Ireland a mere turf bank is called a hedge.

December

George is a man plagued by memories that surface so irrepressibly at times that he seems disgruntled. It is not his age – though he is nearly eighty. He sums up his discontent in an oft-repeated phrase as though it were an incantation by means of which he hopes to conjure up the days of yore: 'You see, sir, afore I came home to lend brother Perce a hand, I was a horseman.'

Proud word: a horseman; not simply a carter or ploughman.

I meet George often when he is taking his 'young' brother's cows to and from pasture, and particularly hateful, galling, to him is the main road stretch, a hill to boot, between their farm and a small plot of land nearer the village which they occasionally use.

'Corbugger, 'tis shameful at times', he says, both plaintively and incredulously, as we lean on a gate, looking out across the valley at the woods where a few leaves still wave like defiant banners after the rest have been stripped by the frosts. 'You should hear what they lorry drivers says to me sometimes. They blessed cows. You see, sir, I was a horseman. . .'

Horses: lovely creatures. All horses were *per se* fine, but to George it is above all the working horse that counted. Clydesdales, they were all right; fast workers, could step out smartish. But bad tempered at times. You ask any smith. Suffolk Punches – they had punch all right, not so big, but good solid animals, quiet, too. Even them Frenchies, Percherons, but a bit too high stepping for a work horse. They say they were once upon a time coach horses. Used to see them at the county shows.

But the pick of the bunch, pride o' place, was the Shire horse. He shook his head in slow reminiscence. Biggest, best, heaviest, in the whole wide world. Seventeen hands and more. Hooves bigger'n a man's head. Weighed a ton, almost, did a Shire. A ton of proud horseflesh stepping out along the furrows. But difficult to clean in the legs if you didn't take proper care. Sometimes too much coarse feather that clogged 'em up.

Gazing into the unseen distance, George enthused as eagerly and knowledgeably as if they were Mercedes or Audis. It needs a stretch of imagination for this mechanized generation to visualize that not-so-remote time when the tractor was an exception, the combine harvester barely in existence, the baler an innovation.

Four o'clock every livelong morn we used to get up. And first thing of all we'd water the horses. Always give a horse to drink

The word 'arable' was originally *aerable* and came from the Old English *ear*, to plough. The word 'earth', in this sense, meant the action of ploughing. When these photographs were taken, about fifty years ago, there were two million working horses in Britain. Today there are probably about two thousand. *(ABOVE)* A four-horse team working amid the snow. Such work must have been very hard on both horses and men for ploughing one acre of land entailed covering a total of eleven miles; *(RIGHT)* a three-horse team at work in Wiltshire.

before you feed 'un. If you do it t'other way round, his food'll maybe swell up inside him. A horse an't like a cow with all they girt stomachs she goes on packing the food into. A horse be finer made, got a delicate inside, so you've got to feed 'un slow – little and often – that's why we have nosebags, zno. But they got to have plenty to keep up their strength. A Shire, he'd need a stone or more of crushed oats every day, same again of chopped hay mixed up with the oats so as to make him eat slowly. And roots, too, on top of that – swedes were best.

And you should'a seen the sheen on they horses! There's many a housewife didn't get the same bloom on her furniture as we got on to them, grooming, grooming, we were always at it. Some of the other horsemen where I worked had secret recipes of herbs they'd put into their horses' bait to improve their coats. And I heard of one chap who wiped his horse over with a paraffin rag – said it kept the flies away, too. But 'twas the dandy brush and the curry comb that mattered most. And the brasses, too! We had half a dozen teams where I worked and it was like lightning flashing if they all turned at the headlands at the same time, the brasses were kept so brilliant! Not like they useless things they got nailed up on the beam of the pub!

Horses! The old man's memories were so intense he almost made you hear the majestic tramp of their hooves.

Before the war I drove a trap like this in various parts of the country. I would hesitate to do so nowadays.

'They're coming back, George,' I said, interrupting his reverie, and he looked round sharply, wondering for a moment if 'they blessed cows' had grown impatient and were wending their own way home. 'Work horses. There's even a special school been started up in Gloucestershire for handling work horses. More and more farmers are taking to them again. With petrol and oil getting more and more expensive and more and more difficult, people are turning back to horsepower.'

Ha! He snorted a little at the notion of a special school, but his pale blue eyes glinted as if he had caught a glimpse of the promised land that lay in the past. Slower nor tractors, maybe, but if there was enough of 'em again ... And twenty years they're good for work. Besides, this added slyly, look at the muck. You don't get no dung from tractors, eh? Horse-dung, 'tis marvellous if you don't use 'un too fresh when the ammonia's strong in it!

Well, shall we one day be forced willy nilly back into George's earthy past, with steam-trains run by unlimited coal, windmills whirling in the god-given winds, looms treadled by the feet of craftsmen instead of by computers, ponies and traps on the roads, bicycles in the streets, and horses ploughing the land? Or have we become too punch-drunk trying to get to the stars? Or are there simply too many of us to make George's world possible again?

*

A few fields away from here there is an abandoned stone quarry. I go there often, sometimes into the quarry itself along the overgrown track still smudgily rutted by the work-traffic of years ago, sometimes from above, to sit as near as I dare to the grim lip, among the junipers, hawthorns, blackthorns, hazels, sycamores and wayfaring trees and elders, hollies, rowans and scrubby little oaks and all the other members of this natural arboretum that have sprung up along the top of the sheer quarry-cliff. A rickety fence protects them from the cows on the fieldside who go down on their knees to snatch a mouthful of grass from under the lowest strand of barbed wire.

Down below, honeysuckle and willow-herb take turns in erecting a canopy over the wrecks of ancient vehicles. Rust has even taken a hand improving the place, for here and there among the thickets of brambles and nettles are gaudy patches of orange-red corrugated iron that crumbles at a touch or a derelict water-tank. The slate roofs of the worksheds have fallen in and in autumn grey plumes of old man's beard issue from the chimney stacks instead of smoke. Out of a broken window protrudes an enormous round bunch of ivy, like the head of some grotesque 'green man' surveying the morning.

Those tumbledown buildings and their attendant rampant bushes are a community centre for nesting birds – robins, blackbirds, thrushes, tits, wrens, dunnocks, spotted flycatchers, warblers, house-martins, all build there. A ruined boiler has a tenant, too. In spring-time you could rarely find a more concentrated chorus of bird-song, which is thrown back by the rock-face, so that there seem to be ten times as many joyful voices as there truly are.

There are larger residents, too. Two hen pheasants, attended by a cock bird, frequent the place and certainly nest there, for I have come across the remnants of egg-shells. If you are down in the quarry and the three birds go rocketing overhead, the cock hiccuping in the rear, they look as big as capercaillies against the sky. In the niches and ledges of the elephant-grey precipice jackdaws nest and have as neighbours a pair of kestrels. The male bird's eyelash-thin *kee-lee kee-lee* is his equivalent of a song. Sometimes you can see the kestrel and one or two jackdaws perched almost side by side on a branch or an overhead wire.

The guelder-rose (*Virburnum opulus*) originally took its name from the Dutch province of Guelderland.

But the jackdaws are not so tolerant towards any buzzard that comes foraging. And their shrill mobbing is often the signal for the appearance of a pair of ravens which nest down in the valley. Almost invariably, if a buzzard is around, the ravens are close by and vice versa. They may have a mutual antipathy but they are frequent companions; the buzzards mew querulously as they dodge the corvine dive-bombing, while the sonorous *glog glog glog* of the ravens clearly means Out! Out!

In one way or another the quarry and its immediate surroundings must be virtually self-sufficient for many creatures. In good seasons there is an abundance of wild fruits, mostly tantalizingly inaccessible to cumbersome humans. The rowans with their jewel-like berries lean out over the sinister cliff, trying to tempt one fatally; the sloes with their faint bloom are plumper than any within reach; the blackberries are almost fictitiously opulent, and wasps and greenbottles embrace them affectionately. The wild roses whose garlands hung on all sides have turned into fat, polished hips that would make any amount of jelly. Looking down on the peggles of the hawthorns you see a mass of red never properly appreciated from below when you are staring into the light. As for the hazel-nuts, the extent to which they are appreciated is shown by the incredible debris of shells often left in corners of the ruined buildings by bank-voles and dormice.

For those of different tastes there is plenty, too, for the quarry becomes crowded with docks and thistles and yellow poppies, whose seed-heads bring down gay little charms of goldfinches, sometimes accompanied by a pair or two of bullfinches. Ragwort and nettles attract scores of red admirals and tortoiseshells. Ant-hills pock the ground here and there, bringing the occasional visit of a green woodpecker to flaunt his brilliance and make the quarry ring with his splendid laugh.

There is drink as well as food. Except in times of drought, a wispy scarf of water trickles and plashes and murmurs down the grey cliff, and part of the quarry bottom is covered by a dark, fairy-looking lake where yellow flags, water crowfoot and forget-me-not have taken hold. In springtime innumerable frogs render thanks in guttural tones, for near the margins of the water there abound many beautiful snails and less beautiful slugs, brown monsters some of them, but this is well known also to various hedgehogs, while a song-thrush has his anvil near by.

In the willow-tangle a pair of moorhens skulk and punctuate the silence with their loud metallic calls – it was perhaps one of these which, a month or two ago, I found lying dead in the field near the house: in spring and autumn moorhens go on strange, inexplicable night-flights and this bird had evidently blundered into an overhead cable. Wild mallard come to the quarry lake, too, but it is I who am usually surprised by them, for nearly always when I catch sight of them they are in the act of taking off, with 'wings linked and necks astrain'. Once one summer morning a solitary turtle-dove was drinking at the water's edge, where often scores of bees come to sip.

Once, too, while the ghastly baying of hounds rang out in the near-distance, punctuated by a brassy horn I watched a fox creeping along a ledge on the far side of the curving rock-face. How he got there, how he managed to move along such a narrow foothold, I don't know. But he was well acquainted with his sanctuary. He vanished from my field of vision and presently a couple of hounds appeared among the scrub at the edge of the precipice. They stared out uncertainly over the quarry, then suddenly became aware of my presence. With a wuff of surprise, they flinched away, colliding with each other, and then turned tail and made off, seeking reassurance in numbers, and eventually the blaring din of the hunt receded, making me hope my fox was safe.

The quarry is a perfect example of how thoroughly Nature heals the scars left by man – and in so doing makes a place more beautiful than ever it was before. It is also a nature reserve in miniature, covering perhaps three acres. But you don't need anything like that area to encourage nature in one form or another – the corner of a field left unploughed where the brambles are allowed to take over, a clump of saplings allowed to flourish, even a forgotten pile of hedge-trimmings will be taken over as a nesting-site; a tree-stump will become the abode of residents as varied as beefsteak fungus and horntails; slow-worms will harbour under a piece of old iron, wrens and blue tits

will shelter in your nesting-boxes in winter just as gladly as they will use them for their appointed purpose in spring. And, if your garden is big enough, you can always rationalize your laziness by leaving a patch untended. Nature will colonize it and give you pleasure – though, depending where you live, you may have to mollify your neighbour if he complains about the weeds.

⁎

Whenever I go into churchyards which, it must be admitted, is far more often than I attend church, though the bells are sometimes difficult to resist, it does not seem to me that they 'yawn and hell itself breathes out Contagion to this world' – as Hamlet put it.

A Kent farmstead in winter. This is the sort of place one might expect a yeoman farmer to own. However, the word 'yeoman' in mediaeval times, meant any sort of countryman of the middling classes, usually a farmer, but sometimes a servant or even an armed retainer. The idea that a yeoman must be a freeholder arose much later.

Tranquillity and inevitability, the transience of life, the futility and tragedy of human effort, all these, maybe, occur to one strolling among the silent invisible presences symbolized by the grey, lichen-stippled headstones, which are rather like eternal bed-heads, while from the church itself the organ murmurs out its requiem for them all.

But though there is a fascinating compulsion in reading the names and dates of these rude forefathers — their epitaphs, which range from the terse to the flowery and from the sickly pious to the outright comic — in trying to envisage their distant lives — and in admiring the often superbly elegant letter-carving and the dignified stones themselves, all so infinitely more attractive than present-day marble — it is for a churchyard's yews that I look.

Yews line the pathway from lychgate to west door at Hambleden, Buckinghamshire.

Old Yew, which graspest at the stones
That name the under-lying dead,
Thy fibres net the dreamless head,
Thy roots are wrapt about the bones

    Alfred, Lord Tennyson: *In Memoriam*

Some churchyards have none at all, others one or two, some a whole avenue from lychgate to west door, while a Painswick has a round hundred – though such are merely ornamental in origin. The yew is often associated with death because it does occur in graveyards, but that is not its raison d'etre. The churchyard yew is part of England's history, and, much as I detest war, I cannot help thinking of the time when England's chief and most devastating armament was the longbow and under Edward III, the Black Prince and Henry V we possessed the most doughty fighting force in Europe. The crossbow was a murderous weapon, its use forbidden at one time by the Church, but though it had fearful penetration and precision, it was unhandy in practice. A longbowman could loose off six or seven arrows a minute against one or two bolts or 'quarrels' from the cross-bowman.

In those days the yew had by law to be planted in every parish, and the churchyard was the obvious place for this; equally, every able-bodied man and youth was required to practise archery at the butts. When the gun came into fashion the longbow was abandoned, prematurely, for it was a long time before fire-arms became truly effective. We could have retained the rapid fire of the grey goose shaft for another century – instead of which in adopting the cumbersome and imperfect gun we descended to the level of other countries' soldiery. The mechanism of the first portable fire-arm was so complicated that a man was far too preoccupied coping with shot, priming powder and slow match to take careful aim.

The English, or the Welsh, bowman had a technique which French and Scottish archers never mastered. The expression 'to draw a bow' was inaccurate if applied to the English bowman. As W. Gilpin explained in *Remarks on Forest Scenes* (1791): 'The Englishman did not keep his left hand steady, and draw his bow with his right; but (while) keeping his right hand at rest upon the nerve, he pressed the whole weight of his body into the horns of his bow. Hence probably arose the phrase "bending a bow" and the French of "drawing" one.'

So, albeit peaceloving, I cannot help regarding with affection this rock-hard, rock-solid, sturdy tree – but not simply for its historical associations. It is a magnificent creation in itself, with its sometimes horizontal branches whose tips droop to the earth, its massive, many-pillared, iron-red trunk which resembles the clustered columns of cathedral or church, its beautiful pink-red berries, adored by thrushes and blackbirds which feast on them greedily and stain the grass with evidence of their gluttony; the birds do not eat the dark green stones, which are poisonous, as are the leaves of the yew.

Ironically, the yew is coniferous and should technically be a softwood. In fact, it is one of the hardest of timbers, slow growing, and reaching an age of many hundreds of years. Some trees are reputed to be a thousand or more years old. Whether or not the past was 'dreadful', these churchyard yews are certainly 'portions and parcels' of it.

✳

A winter scene subtitled 'Where no Vultures Fly', or 'Pecking Order'. After Mr Maddowcroft had moved his flock from the field nearest the house, one dead sheep was left in the middle of it; it seemed redolent of the frore weather that had descended. As soon as daylight broke it was the scene of much to-ing and fro-ing as sundry avian undertakers came to measure up the corpse. Fourteen magpies, six carrion crows, and a pair of ravens

In the days before myxomatosis drastically reduced the rabbit population, ferreting was a traditional Boxing Day sport for farmers and their men as well as for countryfolk in general. The ferret is placed behind the net into the rabbit hole. As he returns the ferret is caught with the right hand and the netted rabbit is caught with the left.

were gathered round in appreciation of the bounty and it was soon evident that the work had already been put in hand.

It was the ravens who were doing most of the tough preliminary chore and characteristically they had started on the rear end of the sheep. The magpies were walking up and down, flirting their tails and uttering knowing cries like so many consultants asked for their opinion – but in reality waiting to seize their opportunity when the ravens had unlocked the door of the feast. One of the crows sat on the sheep's head, huddled and disconsolate; it had no doubt pecked out one of the eyes but couldn't get at the other.

The magpies became impatient and swarmed round in a never-ending parade, closer still. The ravens became either apprehensive or vexed by all this and constantly backed out hurriedly to check what was going on behind them, whereupon the magpies jumped out of range, only to begin crowding closer again. Magnificent in the air, the ravens on the ground were extraordinarily bandy-legged, but their beards were quite imposing. When they were working they often braced themselves on one leg and wrenched the flesh away with savage urgency. They looked huge in comparison with the slim and jaunty magpies.

In due course the magpies had their turn when the ravens swaggered away to take a breather. All at once the crows, who had resigned themselves to a long wait while the ravens were in possession, realized the magpies had pulled a fast one. Shouting with raucous indignation (no doubt in the avian equivalent of trawlerman's language) they came winging back en masse and there was an explosion of magpies as they scattered before the black onslaught.

But the triumph of the crows did not last long. A new undertaker had arrived on the scene in the shape of a herring-gull. It made no particularly menacing move, just stood there –

When the land was fat with rabbits, their young was the favourite prey of buzzards, especially at nesting-time. But small rodents, beetles, caterpillars, earthworms and, of course, carrion are all included in the buzzard's diet.

and presently slowly advanced towards the carcase. Though the magpies strutted up and down close by as if courteously ushering the gull to the banquet, the crows barked anxiously and gave way. The newcomer set to work with the uncouth directness of somebody prepared to put his boots on the table if necessary. The crows proceeded to work off their discomfiture by mobbing a buzzard which had turned up and was cravenly waiting at least fifty yards away.

The demolition work went on all day. Green plovers and redwings crowded the field round about, oblivious to the rather coarse goings-on, though the plovers wailed angrily when occasionally the waiting magpies vented their spite on them. By next morning the rib cage of the defunct ewe was well exposed and at times the ravens vanished out of sight inside the carcase. This clearly was a messy job and one of the ravens waddled away and began vigorously cleaning its beak on the grass, wiping it from side to side. Then it twice wrenched out tufts of grass and soil and, craning its neck, dropped these over its back. This was not enough: it flattened right down on the ground and gave its body a thorough rubbing in the grass, almost rolling over completely in the strenuous process of cleaning itself.

The magpies were so intrigued by this that those at the back of the queue gathered round the raven and started teasing it. Several times as it squatted there it had to duck as a magpie buzzed it, *lèse-majesté* if ever there was. Both the ravens, now surely suitably gorged, went off to some nearby ivy-clad ash-trees and spent a long time eating berries, as dessert perhaps.

The first time the buzzard plucked up courage to come on to the carcase was when everyone else had departed and a frosty dusk was drawing down the blinds.

That evening I went out with a torch and green eyes glowed at me momentarily as a fox swung away. At daybreak I visited the carcase again (skeleton rather, by now) and a rat scurried out of it and humpled across the field. At the end of the third day nothing remained of the sheep but scattered wool and a few bare ribs that looked like the wreck of a boat stranded long ago. Even the skull and larger bones had been carried off by foxes and prowling dogs.

It had indeed been a movable feast.

✳

Avian Jekyll and Hyde: for weeks on end, mainly in the mornings, a kestrel has taken up his lookout on an overhead wire a few yards outside the garden fence; occasionally closer still on one of the posts of the washing-line. It is a male, because it has a blue-grey head and tail (with a distinctive black bar at the end) and chestnut back; the female's back is more rufous, her head less proudly hooded.

The kestrel by no means always hunts with that characteristic and delightful action that has given him another name, 'Wind-hover'. When he hunts in this way he hangs some forty feet above the earth, 'standing' in the air with quivering wings and out-spread, depressed tail keeping his balance, waiting to pounce down on shrew or field-vole or mouse – which gave rise to yet another name: Mouse-hawk. (Seton Gordon recorded a family of kestrels eating more than ten thousand mice in 210 days.)

That hovering, delicately balanced, supremely skilful action is one of the most marvellous sights in nature. It is perfected uniquely by the kestrel, being matched by no other bird of prey, even though some other species do attempt a cumbersome form of hovering at times. Yet the kestrel, if he has a handy lookout, such as I have mentioned, does not waste energy in hovering. He justs sits on his perch, keenly, minutely, watching (watch him crane his neck) for beetle or vole and then goes floating gently down at an angle to seize it.

He seems so demure for a hawk (modestly conscious perhaps of his mediaeval antecedents, when, in the heyday of falconry, he was considered fit for knaves and servants to fly), and most of the time other birds appear to take the same view. The visitors to the nearby bird-table ignore him blissfully as he sits on the post a couple of yards outside the garden gate. The robins bob and flirt

A hovering kestrel. Garth Christian referred to a kestrel that was so regular in its midday hunting that he got into the habit of leaving home at a particular time, knowing that he was virtually certain to see it seeking its prey. Wild birds of all kinds appear to have an innate sense of time, as anyone with a bird-table will have noticed.